FOR SUCH A TIME AS THIS

Rising To The Challenge:

Navigating The Present With Purpose

Helen Cummings-Henry

All the scripture quotations are taken from the King James Version.

Paperback: ISBN 978-2-7541-3475-0
ebook: ISBN 978-2-6934-6190-0

Contents

Introduction

For such a time as this' has been widely used to convey the idea that individuals may find themselves in certain situations for a divine purpose or appointed moment."

I am truly grateful for the divine inspiration that guided me in crafting these pages and bringing this book to fruition. As you embark on this spiritual journey, I believe it is not by chance that you are here but by divine appointment. The pages you are about to read are more than words; they are an invitation to explore the depths of faith, purpose, and connection with God.

I invite you to approach these pages with an open heart, ready to receive the blessings of divine insight and wisdom. May this book be a source of inspiration, comfort, and life-changing power in your life. As you read, may you sense the presence of the Divine, guiding you on your own unique path.

Welcome to "For Such a Time As This: Rising to the Challenge: Navigating the Present with Purpose," a heartfelt exploration of navigating life's intricate dance with a divine touch.

This book is more than a mere guide; it's an invitation to explore the interplay between our human journey and the divine presence that colors every facet of our existence. It's a recognition that amidst the turbulence of these times, there exists a steadfast anchor—an unwavering connection to something greater than ourselves.

The title echoes a timeless truth, drawing from a wisdom that transcends eras: that each moment, no matter how daunting, carries within it the seeds of purpose. It's an acknowledgment that we are called, in our own unique ways, to rise, confront challenges, and navigate this chapter of history with resilience, wisdom, and a profound alignment with the divine.

Within these pages, we embark on a journey that not only illuminates strategies for overcoming obstacles but also celebrates the role of faith and spirituality in guiding our paths. It's an exploration of how our connection with God, however we perceive or name that higher power, serves as a beacon, illuminating the darkest paths and infusing our steps with purpose and meaning.

As we delve into strategies, insights, and reflections, let us remember that this journey is not solitary; it's a collective pilgrimage toward deeper understanding and purposeful living. May this book serve as a conduit, connecting our aspirations with divine guidance, and inspiring us to navigate these times with grace, conviction, and an unwavering connection to the divine presence that sustains us.

In the canvas of human history, there are moments when the threads of fate seem to weave a unique tapestry of challenges and opportunities. It's during these junctures that the essence of our beliefs, our values, and our faith is put to the test. "For Such a Time As This: Rising to the Challenge: Navigating the Present with Purpose" stands as a testament to the enduring power of faith amidst the tumultuous seas of change.

This book doesn't just acknowledge the existence of God as an abstract notion; it celebrates the divine presence as a guiding force, an ever-present companion in our journey through life's highs and lows. It's an ode to the belief that, in acknowledging and aligning with this higher power, we find strength, resilience, and a sense of purpose that transcends the transient nature of our worldly challenges.

As we traverse the landscapes of uncertainty and possibility within these pages, may this exploration ignite a spark of introspection and deepen our connection to something greater.

Together, let's embrace this opportunity to navigate the present with a profound understanding of our divine purpose, drawing strength from our faith to illuminate the path ahead. This journey isn't just about facing challenges; it's about embodying a purposeful existence, guided by faith, and leaving an indelible mark of positivity and compassion in the sands of time.

Thank you for being a part of this sacred journey. May your reading experience be filled with moments of enlightenment, and may the words written here resonate deeply within your spirit. May you discover, within these pages, the divine appointment that brought you here and the purpose that awaits you on the other side.

CHAPTER ONE

Divine Insight

For the Lord giveth wisdom: out of his mouth cometh knowledge and understanding."
− Proverbs 2:6

IN THE LABYRINTH OF LIFE'S UNCERTAINTIES, FAITH becomes your guiding star, illuminating the path obscured by doubts and fears.

It's not merely a passive belief but an active force that propels you forward, even when the way ahead seems shrouded in obscurity.

This faith, a profound trust in God's guidance, anchors you amidst the tempest of uncertainties, offering solace and direction when your human understanding falters.

When the horizon appears hazy, and decisions loom like uncharted territories, faith in action becomes your compass.

It's a deliberate surrender, a conscious choice to trust in a higher wisdom that surpasses your own. This trust isn't blind; it's a belief in divine orchestration, an assurance that even in chaos, a meticulous plan unfolding with purpose and grace exists.

Amidst life's upheavals, this faith transforms into a resilient stance—a steadfast conviction that even amid adversity, there's a benevolent force guiding your steps.

It's the unwavering confidence that every twist, every turn, and every obstacle holds within it a lesson, a blessing, or an opportunity for growth.

To trust God's guidance amidst uncertainty isn't to evade challenges but to confront them with an unwavering belief that you are not alone in this journey.

It's an acknowledgment that your human limitations meet their match in divine omnipotence, and that intersection births a synergy capable of steering you through the stormiest seas.

In this act of trust, there's liberation. It liberates you from the paralyzing grip of doubt, allowing you to move forward with a sense of purpose and courage.

It's an invitation to lean into the unknown, confident that the hands steering your ship are steady, wise, and infinitely compassionate.

In the tapestry of existence, your understanding of the times finds depth and clarity through a divine perspective—a lens that transcends the temporal and delves into the spiritual essence of your journey.

It's a perspective nurtured by faith, one that perceives events not merely as isolated incidents but as threads interwoven into a larger, purposeful design.

When you embrace a divine perspective, the chaotic becomes coherent, the mundane turns meaningful, and the obscure finds illumination.

It's an acknowledgment that beyond the surface of events lies a profound tapestry orchestrated by a higher intelligence—a narrative that unfolds with purpose and intentionality.

Faith, as the conduit to this divine perspective, enables you to see beyond the veil of immediacy, inviting you to contemplate the deeper significance of each moment.

It's an invitation to perceive trials not as stumbling blocks but as stepping stones, recognizing that within adversity, there exists an opportunity for spiritual growth and resilience.

This perspective isn't shielded from the complexities of existence; rather, it embraces them, acknowledging that even during challenges, there exists a divine order, a harmonious symphony playing out in the seemingly discordant notes of life.

It's the lens through which we discern meaning in the seemingly mundane and beauty during chaos.

Understanding the times through faith's lens isn't about escapism but about engaging with reality at a deeper level—one that acknowledges the divine hand guiding every moment, infusing your experiences with purpose and significance.

It's an empowering realization that in your journey through life, every chapter, every twist, and every turn contribute to a greater narrative—one that transcends our transient existence.

In the realm of spiritual exploration, divine insight stands as a beacon illuminating the path to understanding beyond the confines of the tangible world.

It's more than just knowledge; it's a profound understanding that transcends the limitations of your senses, offering glimpses into the profound mysteries of existence.

Divine insight is often the fruit of a deep communion with the divine—an intimate connection that opens the floodgates of wisdom and revelation.

It's the kind of insight that doesn't merely scratch the surface but delves into the depths of the soul, bringing forth revelations that reshape perspectives and transform lives.

This form of insight isn't confined to the pious or the devout; it's a gift available to all who seek it with an open heart and a receptive mind.

It's an invitation to pause, to listen to the whispers of the universe, and to tap into a reservoir of wisdom that transcends the boundaries of human understanding.

When divine insight graces your consciousness, it's as if a veil is lifted, revealing truths that were once obscured.

It offers clarity that cuts through the fog of confusion, granting you a panoramic view of your life and the world around you. This clarity isn't just intellectual; it's a profound inner knowing—a conviction that comes not from logic alone but from a deep resonance within the core of your being.

Embracing divine insight isn't about acquiring esoteric knowledge; it's a transformative journey that reshapes your perceptions and fuels your spiritual evolution.

It's an ongoing quest to seek deeper truths, to live authentically, and to walk a path illuminated by the radiant light of divine wisdom.

In the tumultuous seasons of my life, it was the anchor of faith that held me steady and allowed me to navigate the stormy waters with a divine perspective.

One vivid memory etched in my heart is from a time of profound uncertainty and personal tribulation.

I found myself standing at the crossroads of a major life decision, unsure of which path to tread.

It was then that I turned to prayer, seeking guidance and solace in the quiet moments of communion with the divine.

As I immersed myself in prayerful contemplation, a profound sense of peace enveloped me.

It was as if the divine presence whispered assurances, assuring me that even in the face of uncertainty, there existed a purposeful plan unfolding.

This experience marked a pivotal shift in my understanding of faith—it wasn't merely a passive belief but an active engagement with the divine, seeking understanding and guidance in the complexities of life.

The divine perspective became even more evident as time unfolded. The challenges I faced weren't eradicated, but my perception of them transformed.

I began to see each obstacle as an opportunity for growth, and every setback as a stepping stone towards a higher purpose.

It was through this lens of faith that I started to understand that the divine perspective isn't about escaping difficulties but embracing them with the unwavering belief that they contribute to a grander narrative.

In moments of distress, I clung to a verse that resonated deeply: "For I know the plans I have for you, plans to prosper you and not to harm you, plans to give you hope and a future."

This promise became a mantra, a source of strength that fortified my spirit. Through the ebb and flow of life's challenges, faith became the lens through which I perceived the unfolding narrative—each chapter intricately woven into the fabric of a greater divine plan.

It wasn't a magic wand that waved away my troubles, but rather a transformative perspective that enabled me to face them with resilience and hope.

The divine perspective, born out of personal struggles and strengthened through faith, became a guiding force, providing clarity, purpose, and a profound sense of connection to something greater than myself.

In embracing this perspective, I discovered that faith not only sustains us through the storms but empowers us to dance in the rain, knowing that even amidst the challenges, there exists a divine order that shapes our journey.

In the crucible of life's trials, my journey has been a testament to the transformative power of faith, embodying the essence of a divine perspective.

There was a period in my life when the shadows of doubt and uncertainty seemed insurmountable. Amidst career upheavals and personal challenges, I found solace in the sanctuary of my faith, a sanctuary that would reshape my outlook on life.

During a particularly trying time, when professional setbacks seemed to overshadow any glimmer of hope, I turned to prayer and sought guidance from a higher power.

It was in those moments of quiet reflection that I felt an overwhelming sense of assurance—an inexplicable peace that transcended the immediate storm.

This was the beginning of my journey toward understanding life through a divine perspective.

As I embraced this newfound faith, I discovered that it wasn't a shield against adversity but a guiding light through it.

One pivotal moment stands out—a moment of unexpected kindness from a stranger during a period of financial strain.

It was as if the universe conspired to demonstrate that even amid challenges, divine provisions can manifest through the kindness of others.

This experience illuminated the notion that a divine perspective doesn't exempt us from difficulties but equips us with the resilience to navigate them.

Through faith's lens, every setback became a stepping stone, every closed door a redirection, and every trial an opportunity for spiritual growth.

This perspective fueled my determination to persist, and to view challenges as opportunities for refinement rather than roadblocks.

With unwavering faith, I began to see the intricate patterns of life's tapestry—a tapestry woven not haphazardly but with purposeful design.

As I reflect on those challenging times, I realize that the divine perspective allowed me to tap into a wellspring of resilience and hope that I never knew existed within me.

Faith became not just a coping mechanism but a source of inspiration, propelling me forward with a renewed sense of purpose.

It's a perspective that continually reminds me that even in the most difficult chapters of our lives, there exists a divine author, crafting a narrative that transcends our limited understanding.

In understanding the times through faith, I have come to appreciate life's uncertainties as invitations to deepen our trust in the divine plan.

Through the lens of faith, our trials become triumphs, our struggles become stepping stones, and our journey becomes a sacred pilgrimage toward a purpose greater than ourselves.

Amidst the ebb and flow of life's complexities, I invite you to consider the transformative power of faith—a journey that encompasses the profound essence of a divine perspective.

In the tapestry of your own experiences, some moments call for a shift in perspective, moments that beckon you to understand the times through the lens of unwavering faith.

In the heart of challenges, envision faith not as a passive bystander but as your staunch ally, empowering you to face uncertainties with courage and resilience. Your life's narrative is an unfolding story, and faith becomes the ink that transforms setbacks into tales of triumph, uncertainties into opportunities, and hardships into stepping stones toward a purpose beyond imagination.

Pause for a moment and reflect on the times when the path ahead seemed shrouded in darkness.

It is precisely in those moments that faith can be your guiding light, casting away shadows and illuminating a way forward.

Consider the divine perspective as a compass that points not only to the destination but also to the beauty of the journey—the twists, the turns, and the unexpected blessings along the way.

As you navigate the complexities of your own story, remember that a divine perspective isn't a shield against challenges but a source of strength that enables you to endure, learn, and grow.

In embracing this perspective, you align yourself with a higher purpose, recognizing that your journey is part of a grander design—an intricate tapestry woven by a benevolent hand.

May this invitation to understand the times through faith resonate deeply within you.

Embrace the power of divine perspective, for in doing so, you embark on a journey of profound self-discovery, purposeful living, and an enduring connection to something greater than the transient nature of life's challenges.

In concluding this chapter on the divine perspective, I am reminded of the profound wisdom encapsulated in the journey of understanding the times through faith.

As we navigate the intricacies of our existence, may we carry with us the resonance of this divine perspective—a perspective that transcends the temporal and connects us to a higher purpose.

The journey toward understanding the times through faith is not a finite exploration but a continual awakening.

It is an ongoing dialogue with the divine, an ever-deepening communion that allows us to perceive the rhythm of life with heightened sensitivity and awareness.

As we stand at the juncture of each moment, may we cultivate the habit of seeking the divine perspective—a perspective that transforms the mundane into the sacred and infuses our experiences with a profound sense of purpose.

Let us remember that faith isn't a static state but a dynamic force that evolves with our experiences and deepens with our commitment.

In embracing a divine perspective, we open ourselves to the vast expanse of possibilities that life presents.

Every challenge becomes an opportunity for spiritual growth, and every triumph is a testament to the grace that guides our journey.

May the divine perspective continue to illuminate your path, offering clarity in moments of confusion, solace in times of distress, and a sense of purpose that transcends the ordinary. Let this understanding be a beacon, guiding you through the pages of your life's unfolding story with grace, resilience, and an unwavering connection to the divine source that sustains us all.

CHAPTER TWO

Faith in Action

"Commit thy works unto the Lord, and thy thoughts shall be established."
— Proverbs 16:3

AMID THE UNCERTAINTY, YOU FIND SOLACE IN THE embrace of faith.

Faith beckons you to a sacred journey, inviting you to navigate the unpredictable terrain of life with a steadfast trust in something greater than yourself.

As you stand at the crossroads of decisions, this chapter becomes your companion, urging you to entrust your path to the divine wisdom that transcends the complexities of the unknown.

In these moments of doubt and ambiguity, you discover the transformative power of faith in action.

It's not merely a passive belief but a deliberate choice to surrender to the guidance of a higher power.

As you delve into the pages, you are encouraged to release the burdens of uncertainty and lean into the assurance that comes from placing your trust in God.

It's a dynamic partnership between your aspirations and the divine orchestrations that shape your journey.

Through the narratives woven within this chapter, you see glimpses of your own experiences reflected.

The challenges you face are not isolated; they are part of a universal tapestry of human existence. In embracing faith, you are not alone.

You join a lineage of believers who, in their own moments of uncertainty, found strength and direction by leaning on the unwavering support of a higher power.

The practical wisdom offered within "Faith in Action" becomes a compass for your decision-making.

It encourages you to draw from the well of faith when confronted with life's dilemmas, fostering a sense of clarity and purpose that transcends the immediate circumstances.

In surrendering to God's guidance, you discover a profound source of resilience that enables you to navigate the ebb and flow of life with grace and confidence.

As you absorb the insights presented in this chapter, you are invited to take tangible steps, infused with faith, toward a future that unfolds in alignment with a divine plan.

It's a call to not only trust but to actively engage your beliefs in shaping the narrative of your life.

In these moments of uncertainty, you find not only a guide but a co-author in the divine, scripting a story of purpose, hope, and unwavering faith.

As you delve deeper into the pages of "Faith in Action", consider the questions that emerge within the narrative.

How does the concept of faith resonate with your own experiences?

Have you encountered moments where uncertainties tested the foundation of your beliefs?

How has faith been a guiding force in navigating the uncertainties that life presents?

What does it mean for you to actively trust God's guidance amid uncertainty?

How can you infuse your decisions with the essence of faith in practical, everyday scenarios?

This book becomes not just a source of information but a catalyst for introspection, urging you to engage in a dialogue with yourself, your beliefs, and your relationship with the divine.

The anecdotes shared within the chapters become invitations to consider your own stories.

Are there instances in your life where, in hindsight, you recognize the subtle hand of providence guiding your steps?

What lessons can be gleaned from those experiences?

The narrative unfolds as a tapestry of questions, inviting you to unravel the threads of your own faith journey and discover the deeper meaning within the complexities of your uncertainties.

As this book encourages you to embrace doubt as an integral part of the faith journey, it poses the question: How can moments of uncertainty serve as catalysts for a more profound connection with the divine?

Can you view challenges not as obstacles to faith but as opportunities for spiritual growth and deeper trust?

The questions woven into each paragraph invite you to reimagine your relationship with uncertainty, encouraging you to see it not as a hindrance but as a pathway to a more vibrant faith.

How will you carry the insights and wisdom gained from this narrative into your own life?

What steps can you take to actively trust God's guidance amid the uncertainties that lie ahead?

The narrative becomes an ongoing conversation, and these questions are the keys that unlock the doors to a more profound understanding of your faith and the active role it can play in shaping your responses to life's uncertainties.

As you grapple with the questions, you will find that the answers are not mere conjectures, but revelations drawn from the very fabric of your own experiences.

Reflecting on the concept of faith, you discover that it resonates deeply with moments when, amidst the tumult of uncertainties, an unwavering belief in something greater provides solace and direction.

Faith, you realize, isn't an abstract notion; it's a lived experience that has shaped the contours of your journey.

The narrative's inquiry into the impact of uncertainties on your beliefs prompts you to acknowledge the times when doubts have indeed tested the foundation of your faith.

Yet, you find that these very challenges have become the crucibles in which your beliefs have been refined, solidified, and ultimately deepened.

Considering the question of how faith guides decisions in practical scenarios, you discern that the essence of faith isn't confined to grand gestures but permeates the ins and outs of daily life.

You recognize that the choices infused with the spirit of trust in the divine often lead to a sense of peace and purpose.

Through these reflections, you uncover that the practical application of faith isn't a distant ideal but an attainable reality that shapes the quality of your decision-making.

The inquiry into instances where the hand of providence may have guided your steps becomes a journey of revelation.

As you revisit pivotal moments, you discern a pattern of grace woven through the tapestry of your life.

The answers emerge from the recognition that, indeed, there have been instances where you felt a guiding presence, steering you through challenges and illuminating the path ahead.

Embracing doubt as a catalyst for a deeper connection with the divine, you uncover that uncertainty isn't antithetical to faith but an integral part of its dynamic nature.

Your answers reveal that moments of doubt have served as opportunities for introspection, fostering a more profound understanding of your beliefs.

Instead of viewing uncertainties as obstacles, you see them as invitations to lean into faith, turning challenges into catalysts for spiritual growth.

In response to the final question about carrying the insights from the narrative into your life, you realize that the wisdom gained isn't meant to be confined to the pages of the book.

Your answers unfold as a commitment—an active decision to integrate the principles of trusting God's guidance into your daily existence.

The narrative becomes a roadmap, and your answers transform into actionable steps, guiding you toward a life where faith is not just a theoretical concept but a lived reality, shaping your responses to the uncertainties that lie ahead.

One pivotal chapter in my life stands out—a crossroads where decisions held weighty consequences, and uncertainty loomed like an ominous cloud.

In those moments, faith wasn't a passive concept but an active force that guided my choices.

Trusting in God's guidance became more than a platitude; it was a lifeline, offering a sense of direction and purpose in the unknown.

Reflecting on past challenges, I see threads of divine intervention subtly woven through the fabric of my experiences.

Instances where serendipity felt more like providence and seemingly insurmountable obstacles gave way to unexpected opportunities.

These personal anecdotes are not just stories; they are testaments to the transformative power of faith in shaping the trajectory of my life.

Yet, my journey isn't a linear progression; it's a tapestry of highs and lows, doubts and certainties.

There have been moments when the echoes of uncertainty drowned out the whispers of faith.

It's in these valleys that the book's narratives became beacons, resonating with my own struggles, offering solace, and reigniting the flame of trust in the divine.

In embracing wisdom, I've come to understand that faith isn't a destination but a continuous journey—a dynamic interplay between my human experience and a guiding force beyond comprehension.

Consider the uncertainties you face, those moments that elicit a subtle hesitation or stir a lingering doubt.

What if, within these very uncertainties, lies the fertile ground for a deeper connection with the divine?

As you read, reflect on your own experiences where faith has played a role in navigating the complexities of decision-making.

How have moments of trust in a higher power shaped the direction of your life?

This narrative is more than a guide; it's a mirror reflecting the contours of your own faith journey, affirming the resilience that surfaces when you actively embrace the principle of faith in your decisions.

Consider the stories shared within the chapters, recognizing that they echo not only the author's experiences but also your own.

How do these narratives resonate with your struggles, victories, and the silent conversations you've had with your own faith?

This book becomes a conversation—a dialogue between the stories within and the story you are actively writing with each passing day.

This is not a passive reading experience but an opportunity for you to engage with the transformative power of faith in your life.

How can the practical insights and reflections within these pages be applied to your own decisions, both big and small?

Take a moment to envision a life where trust in God's guidance becomes not just a philosophy but a tangible force shaping the quality of your daily choices.

As you reach the conclusion of this narrative, consider the lingering resonance of the wisdom imparted.

How will you carry this newfound understanding into the uncertainties that lie ahead?

This book isn't just a temporary guide; it's a compass, directing you toward a future where faith is not just a concept but a lived reality, guiding you through the complexities of your own unique journey.

In drawing this chapter to a close, take a moment to reflect on the tapestry of insights and revelations that have unfolded before you.

These pages have been more than a mere exploration of faith; they have been an intimate journey into the very core of your beliefs and the profound dance with uncertainty.

Consider the threads of thought that have woven through these pages—each paragraph a brushstroke, painting a vivid picture of trust in God's guidance amid the uncertainties of life.

It's a mirror reflecting the contours of your own experiences, prompting you to see the intersection of your beliefs with the universal themes explored within.

Think about the moments of recognition and resonance, where the stories shared felt like chapters from your own life.

This isn't just a book; it's an invitation to acknowledge the shared humanity in our struggles, victories, and continuous quest for meaning in the face of life's uncertainties.

Let these concluding paragraphs be a bridge—a bridge that connects the wisdom gleaned from these pages with the path that stretches ahead.

It's a call to carry the torch of trust, lighting the way through the uncharted territories that lie beyond this chapter.

The narrative doesn't end here; it merely takes a pause, inviting you to carry the lessons learned into the chapters yet to be written.

Can you envision the transformation that can unfold as you actively incorporate the principles of faith into your daily life?

Picture a future where uncertainties become opportunities for a deeper connection with the divine—a future where trust is not just a response to life's challenges but a guiding force shaping the narrative of your existence.

As you bid farewell to this chapter, let the echoes of faith linger, guiding you into the unwritten pages of the next chapter in your journey.

CHAPTER THREE

Prayerful Decision-Making

If any of you lack wisdom, let him ask of God, that giveth to all men liberally, and upbraideth not; and it shall be given him."
— James 1:5

A S YOU EMBARK ON THE JOURNEY THROUGH THESE pages, envision this chapter not just as a collection of words but as a sanctuary—a space where the intricate dance between prayer and decision-making unfolds.

In the stillness before making decisions, I invite you to pause and consider the transformative power of prayer.

Imagine prayer not merely as a ritual but as a conduit—a channel through which you can seek clarity in the divine wisdom that weaves through the fabric of your existence.

These opening paragraphs become a gentle ushering, guiding you into a space where prayer isn't just an act but a sacred dialogue with the Almighty, a journey to discern the whispers of divine guidance.

As you read, imagine the fullness of your own life, recognizing that the decisions you grapple with are part of a universal tapestry of seeking clarity in the divine counsel.

Prayer takes on a new significance—a deliberate practice that transforms your approach to decision-making.

Envision the decisions ahead not as isolated choices but as threads intricately woven into the larger narrative of your life, each one touched by the grace of prayer.

This chapter is an invitation to integrate prayer seamlessly into your decision-making process, creating a rhythm where every choice is a heartfelt conversation with God, seeking the clarity that can only be found in His wisdom.

As you embrace the idea that this exploration is not just intellectual but experiential.

Imagine the words not merely being read but absorbed, seeping into the very core of your being.

Let this be a catalyst for a transformative shift—a conscious decision to embark on a journey where prayer becomes the cornerstone of clarity in your decisions, shaping your path with divine wisdom.

Envision the act of prayer as more than a mere conversation—it is a sacred dialogue, a communion with the divine where your deepest concerns and uncertainties find resonance.

Let the notion of prayerful decision-making become a beacon, illuminating the path ahead.

Picture the decisions that lie on your horizon infused with the light of God's wisdom, as each prayerful moment becomes a deliberate step toward clarity and purpose.

Consider the practical aspects of prayer in decision-making.

Envision prayer not as a detached ritual but as an intimate involvement with the Almighty—a dynamic engagement where you seek not only answers but a profound understanding of God's will.

Let these paragraphs inspire a shift in your perspective, transforming prayer into a tool that shapes the lens through which you view decisions, allowing divine clarity to permeate even the intricacies of your choices.

Allow the struggles and triumphs of others to become touchstones, resonating with your own journey.

Imagine the potential ripple effect of prayerful decision-making in your life.

Envision decisions no longer clouded by uncertainty but guided by a profound sense of purpose.

See the transformative power of incorporating prayer as an integral part of your decision-making process.

This is a call to action, inviting you to step into a future where prayer becomes not just a momentary pause but a continual rhythm, harmonizing with the divine wisdom that shapes the course of your life.

Let the journey of prayerful decision-making linger in your thoughts.

Picture the continued impact of this exploration, echoing in the decisions that lie ahead.

Embrace the idea that seeking clarity in God's wisdom through prayer is not a finite endeavor but a continuous journey, an ongoing dialogue that shapes the contours of your existence with divine grace and insight.

My own story intricately weaves into the tapestry of shared experiences.

There was a pivotal moment when the weight of a decision seemed insurmountable, and uncertainty cast a shadow on my path.

In the midst of the turmoil, prayer became not just a recourse but a lifeline—an earnest plea for clarity in the divine wisdom that transcends my understanding.

As I reflect on that juncture, I see how prayer transformed the decision-making process.

It wasn't a desperate cry for a specific outcome but a surrender—an acknowledgment that I needed guidance beyond my own capabilities.

The act of prayerful decision-making became a journey inward, a deliberate turning toward the divine for insight, understanding, and clarity that only God could provide.

In the chapters of my life where decisions loomed large, the echoes of those prayers reverberated in the subsequent steps I took.

The unfolding events seemed to align with a higher purpose, offering glimpses of clarity amidst the uncertainties.

It wasn't a miraculous resolution of every challenge, but rather a subtle shift in perspective—a recognition that, through prayer, decisions became opportunities for a deeper connection with God's wisdom.

There were moments when my prayers seemed to be met with silence, leaving me in the throes of doubt.

Yet, as I continued to engage in prayerful decision-making, the silence became a canvas for trust to flourish.

It became a journey of understanding that God's timing and plans often transcend my immediate comprehension, and the clarity sought may unfold in ways unforeseen.

This chapter serves as a reminder that my story is not isolated but part of a broader narrative—a narrative that echoes the struggles, victories, and lessons learned by others who have tread similar paths.

Through prayerful decision-making, I discovered a profound interconnectedness with the collective human experience, finding solace in the shared journey toward clarity in God's wisdom.

Allow God's words to unfold before you like a sacred scroll.

Consider the decisions looming on your horizon—the weight they carry, the uncertainties they veil.

Now, envision prayer not as a distant ritual but as a profound tool within your reach.

In the act of prayerful decision-making, you are not alone.

These paragraphs extend a hand, inviting you to immerse yourself in the transformative journey where the divine and your choices entwine.

As you navigate the practicalities of decision-making, envision prayer becoming a dynamic force, shaping the lens through which you view your choices.

Picture each prayer as a sacred brushstroke, illuminating the path with divine clarity.

This is an invitation to actively engage with your faith, allowing it to permeate not just your spiritual life but every facet of your decision-making process.

Let these words inspire a shift in perspective—a recognition that prayerful decision-making is not a complex endeavor but a simple, heartfelt dialogue with God.

It's an opportunity to share your hopes, fears, and aspirations openly, trusting that in the divine wisdom sought, clarity will unfold like the petals of a blossoming flower.

In the mosaic of experiences shared within these pages, recognize your own reflection.

Consider these words not as mere ink on paper but as a resonant melody, harmonizing with the rhythms of your own life, beckoning you toward a future where decisions are bathed in the luminosity of God's wisdom.

As you continue to absorb the essence of this thought let it be more than a reading experience—let it be a catalyst for action.

Envision a life where prayerful decision-making becomes second nature, where seeking clarity in God's wisdom is not an occasional practice but an integral part of your daily rhythm.

In your sacred sanctuary, hear the resonance of God's peace as a soul-stirring symphony, uniquely composed for you.

Envision each word as a vibrant note, harmonizing with the cadence of your own spiritual journey.

Allow the wisdom shared to be a guiding melody that echoes in the chambers of your heart.

Picture the decisions that currently weigh on your mind—the crossroads that beckon for your attention.

Now, imagine prayer as not just a ritual but a transformative conversation, a divine dialogue where you lay bare your uncertainties, hopes, and dreams.

Inviting you to infuse your decision-making with the sacred energy of prayer.

In the practicalities of your daily life, let God become a Beacon, guiding you to view decisions as opportunities for spiritual communion.

Envision the integration of prayer into your decision-making process as a seamless dance, where each step is a rhythm attuned to the divine guidance that permeates your choices.

As you absorb the inspired Wisdom of God, see it not as a fleeting moment of insight but as a transformative catalyst for change.

Envision a future where prayerful decision-making becomes a cornerstone of your daily routine, where seeking divine clarity is not just a response to challenges but a conscious, proactive choice in every decision you make.

Feel the gentle nudge to embrace a deeper connection with the divine—a connection that transcends the boundaries of the written words and becomes a living, breathing presence in your life.

Picture each prayer as a stepping stone, guiding you towards a horizon where decisions are bathed in the radiant glow of God's wisdom, leading you to a life of purpose, assurance, and unwavering clarity.

In these closing sentences, envision the wisdom shared not as a finite resource but as an eternal spring—an ever-flowing well of inspiration that you can return to whenever the complexities of decision-making arise.

Let it be a reminder that the journey of seeking clarity in God's wisdom is not confined to the pages of a book but extends into the infinite possibilities of your ongoing relationship with the divine.

As we bid farewell to this chapter, picture the decisions that await you in the future.

Let these words be a touchstone, a guiding light that illuminates the path ahead.

See each decision as an opportunity for prayerful communion, a chance to dance with the divine in a harmonious rhythm where clarity emerges from the sacred dialogue.

Let it permeate your choices, infusing them with a wisdom that transcends human understanding.

As we draw the curtain on this chapter, envision the ripple effect of your choices infused with divine clarity.

Let it extend beyond your immediate sphere, touching the lives of those around you.

May this not be an isolated exploration but a catalyst for a more profound connection with the divine in every decision you make.

In the stillness that follows, carry the resonance of prayerful decision-making with you, allowing it to frame the story of your life with purpose, insight, and unwavering trust in God's wisdom.

CHAPTER FOUR

Putting God First

*But seek ye first the kingdom of God, and His righteousness, and all
these things shall be added unto you."*
− Matthew 6:33

CONSIDER THE MOMENTS WHEN LIFE'S PRIORITIES seem like a jigsaw puzzle, each piece vying for attention.

In this chapter, allow the narrative to gently prod you, encouraging you to rearrange the pieces of your life according to the divine blueprint.

Picture God not as an addition to your priorities but as the very foundation upon which a purposeful life is built.

Imagine the challenges and triumphs narrated within these pages not as distant tales but as mirrors reflecting your own journey.

See your experiences mirrored in the stories shared, affirming that the quest to put God first is a universal pursuit.

Amid life's hustle, allow God to become your quiet sanctuary—a place for reflection.

Picture yourself in this sacred space, contemplating the profound truth that putting God first is not a burdensome obligation but a liberating choice.

As you bask in the essence of putting God first, let it be more than a theoretical concept.

Picture the blueprint transforming into a living reality, shaping your decisions, relationships, and aspirations.

These are not just words on a page; they are a call to action—a summons to align your life with the divine blueprint, making God the true center of your existence.

Let these words resonate with the beating of your own heart, inviting you to delve deeper into the concept of making God the anchor of your life.

Imagine having a conversation—a dialogue between you and the divine, a discourse that unfolds within the pages of this blueprint.

Visualize each word as a brushstroke, painting a vivid picture of what it means to center your life around God.

God is not distant; He is a present, guiding force, intricately woven into the details of your daily existence.

Consider the complexities of decision-making in your life.

Picture the divine blueprint as a compass, directing your choices with a clarity that transcends worldly concerns.

As you read these words, allow the blueprint to be more than an idea—it's a practical guide, offering a pathway to align your decisions with God's will, making each choice a testament to the priority you give to the divine.

Envision the relationships in your life transforming as you embrace the blueprint of putting God first.

This is a Divine invitation to view your interactions through a lens of love, compassion, and understanding—attributes, that emanate from a life centered on God.

Picture the ripple effect of this shift, not only in your own well-being but in the connections, you foster with others.

In the hustle and bustle of your daily routine, take a sacred pause—a moment to reevaluate the pursuits that occupy your time and energy.

Image yourself in this reflective space, contemplating how your priorities align with the divine blueprint.

In these moments, allow the essence of putting God first to seep into the nooks and crannies of your life, transforming the mundane into the sacred.

As the blueprint unfolds, see it not as a rigid structure but as a dynamic guide that adapts to the ever-changing seasons of your life.

God's presence is not confined to a particular phase; it's a constant, an unwavering center around which the chapters of your life revolve.

Let this blueprint be an enduring compass, directing you towards a life where God's priority becomes not just a concept but the true center of your existence.

In the quiet contemplation of putting God first, let these probing questions become mirrors reflecting the landscape of your priorities and the alignment of your life with the divine blueprint.

As you absorb the words, consider the daily rhythms of your life.

Are your actions and choices orchestrated by a conscious effort to place God at the forefront, or do the demands of the world drown out the divine whispers?

Picture the moments when your decisions take center stage.

How often do you consult the divine blueprint, allowing it to shape the course of your choices?

In the tapestry of your relationships, ask yourself: are they woven with threads of love, forgiveness, and compassion that resonate with a life centered on God?

Consider the people you encounter.

Do you view them through the lens of the divine blueprint, recognizing the inherent worth and dignity in each individual as a reflection of God's creation?

Examine the ambitions and pursuits that occupy your time.

Are they aligned with the eternal purpose outlined in the divine blueprint, or do they prioritize fleeting desires and worldly acclaim?

As you navigate challenges, do you find solace in the divine presence, leaning on the blueprint for guidance, or do you rely solely on human understanding?

In the hustle of your daily routine, probe the recesses of your heart.

How often does the sacred pause, inviting reflection on your priorities, find a place in your busy schedule?

Imagine your life as a canvas.

Do you see the strokes of God's influence and guidance evident in your experiences, decisions, and the overall design of your existence?

Consider the concept of stewardship.

How do you manage the resources entrusted to you—time, talents, and treasures?

Do you approach them with a sense of responsibility, recognizing them as divine gifts outlined in the blueprint for a purposeful life?

As you ponder these questions, let them serve as lanterns illuminating the path towards a life where God is not just a part but the true center, guiding your every step according to His divine blueprint.

Allow me to share a personal story—a testament to the transformative power of aligning one's life with the divine blueprint.

There was a season in my life when the pursuit of worldly success and recognition consumed my priorities.

Every decision I made seemed driven by the desire for accomplishment, and in the process, the divine blueprint took a backseat.

It wasn't until a series of challenges shook the foundations of my carefully constructed life that I realized the emptiness of a path devoid of God's priority.

Amid the uncertainty, I found solace in turning toward the divine blueprint.

My story is not one of an instant transformation but a gradual awakening.

As I immersed myself in prayer, sought wisdom in the scriptures, and consciously placed God at the forefront of my decisions, I witnessed a profound shift.

The divine blueprint became a guiding light, illuminating a purpose that extended beyond personal ambitions.

Through this journey, I discovered the richness of relationships transformed by the divine blueprint. Instead of viewing others as competitors in the race for success, I saw them as fellow travelers on a shared spiritual journey.

Love, compassion, and understanding became the threads that wove the fabric of my interactions, mirroring the divine priorities outlined in the blueprint.

In the realm of decision-making, the divine blueprint became a compass, navigating me through the complexities of life.

As I leaned on God's guidance, choices that once seemed daunting became opportunities for spiritual growth.

The blueprint not only provided clarity in my decisions but also infused a sense of purpose and fulfillment in each step taken.

This personal story serves as a testimony to the profound transformation that occurs when one decides to put God first—a decision that echoes through the chapters of life, shaping every aspect according to the divine blueprint.

It is a journey from a life centered on fleeting achievements to one grounded in eternal purpose—a journey that continues to unfold, guided by the unwavering priority of making God the true center of existence.

Picture yourself standing at the crossroads of your priorities.

What occupies the central space in your life's blueprint?

Is it the pursuit of success, material gain, or perhaps the desire for approval?

Now, consider the transformative power of placing God at the forefront.

How might this shift influence the overall design of your existence?

In the realm of your relationships, envision a tapestry woven with threads of love, kindness, and compassion.

These are the qualities that emerge when God takes His rightful place in the center of your interactions.

Consider the people in your life.

How might your connections deepen when viewed through the lens of the divine blueprint, recognizing the sacredness in each person you encounter?

Reflect on the decisions that shape your daily journey.

How often do you consult the divine blueprint in moments of choice?

Picture the ripple effect of aligning your decisions with God's will. How might this intentional alignment bring clarity, purpose, and a deeper sense of fulfillment to the path you tread?

Think about the moments of solitude and reflection in your life.

Do you intentionally create spaces for a sacred pause, inviting the divine blueprint to speak into the quiet recesses of your heart?

Imagine the profound impact of incorporating such moments into your routine, allowing the priorities outlined in the divine blueprint to permeate every aspect of your being.

Consider the blueprint as a dynamic guide, adapting to the changing seasons of your life.

How might the unwavering presence of God at the center provide a steadying force in the face of life's uncertainties?

Picture a life where God is not merely a part but the true center—a life where every decision, relationship, and pursuit is orchestrated according to His divine blueprint, guiding you toward a purposeful and fulfilling existence.

As we draw near the conclusion of this transformative chapter, let the resonating echoes of divine priorities linger in your thoughts.

These closing words are not a farewell; they are a bridge, inviting you to step into the next chapter with heightened awareness and a renewed commitment to trust God.

Imagine each word as a stepping stone leading you toward the expansive landscape of trust in God.

The foundation laid in prioritizing God is not static; it's a dynamic force that propels you forward.

As we turn the pages to the next chapter, "Trusting God," visualize the divine blueprint seamlessly merging with the principles of trust, creating a tapestry where faith and priorities interlace.

Consider how the blueprint you've crafted in this chapter becomes a vessel—a conduit through which trust flows effortlessly.

Trusting God is not a separate endeavor, but an inherent quality of a life centered on divine priorities.

Picture the trust you've cultivated becoming the pulse that propels every decision, relationship, and aspiration forward, aligned with the eternal principles outlined in the divine blueprint.

In the upcoming chapter, the concept of trust unfolds as a dynamic dance, harmonizing with the priorities you've established.

As we delve into "Trusting God," envisage the dynamic interplay between placing God first and trusting His guidance.

This paragraph is not an ending but a prelude—a glimpse into the synergy of divine priorities and unwavering trust, a dance that propels you into a future brimming with purpose and assurance.

Can you sense the momentum building—a momentum that propels you from the blueprint to trust, creating a continuum of divine principles shaping your life?

As we transition, let these closing thoughts be an encouragement, a dynamic call to embrace the next chapter with an open heart and a resolute commitment to continue placing God at the true center of your life.

CHAPTER FIVE

Trusting God

Trust in the Lord with all thine heart; and lean not unto thine own understanding. In all thy ways acknowledge him, and he shall direct thy paths."
— Proverbs 3:5-6

IN THE LABYRINTH OF LIFE, WHERE UNCERTAINTY casts its formidable shadows, the beacon of trust in God emerges as a guiding light.

Consider the times when the path ahead seemed shrouded in mist, and decisions loomed like daunting challenges.

In this chapter, let the essence of trusting God resonate with your spirit.

Picture trust not as a passive reliance but as an active engagement with the divine, an unwavering belief that even in uncertainty, God's guidance is a steadfast anchor.

Imagine the stories within these pages not as distant anecdotes but as mirrors reflecting your own journey.

Amid uncertainties, how have you experienced the transformative power of trusting God?

As you read these words, let them evoke memories of moments when trust became a lifeline, navigating you through the complexities of life.

Picture trust in God as a dynamic force, shaping your responses to life's twists and turns.

How does the practice of trusting God influence your perspective on challenges?

Envision every uncertainty as an opportunity—an opportunity to lean into the divine guidance that transcends the limitations of human understanding.

In the realm of decision-making, consider the profound impact of trust in God.

How does it influence the choices you make?

Visualize each decision bathed in the brilliance of divine assurance, guided by a trust that surpasses the confines of logic.

Trust is not a passive surrender but an empowering choice—a choice to anchor your decisions in the unwavering belief that God's guidance is sure.

Picture it not as a fleeting emotion but as a foundational principle, an integral part of your spiritual journey.

In the dance with uncertainty, I invite you to step forward with confidence, guided by the surety that trusting God is not just a response to uncertainty but a transformative stance, aligning your path with divine guidance amid life's uncertainties.

Consider the ebb and flow of trust in your life.

How has your trust in God evolved through the various seasons and uncertainties you've encountered?

Envision trust not as a static state but as a river that widens and deepens, carving a path through the landscapes of uncertainty.

Picture the moments when doubts creep in and uncertainties cast their shadows.

How does trust serve as a resilient shield, guarding your spirit against the anxieties that uncertainty can bring?

Let the concept of trust become a beacon, dispelling the darkness, and illuminating a path guided by divine assurance.

In the realm of relationships, reflect on the impact of trust on your connections with others.

How does a foundation of trust transform dynamics, fostering a sense of security and vulnerability?

Envision trust not just as a personal virtue but as a communal force, weaving a tapestry of understanding and support in the face of life's uncertainties.

Imagine trust as a conversation—a continuous dialogue between you and the Divine.

See trust not as a monologue but as a dynamic exchange, a reciprocal dance with God's guidance.

How does this dialogue shape your perspective on uncertainty, transforming it from a source of fear to an opportunity for growth and reliance on God?

Consider the resilience that trust imparts to your spirit.

How does a foundation of trust in God empower you to face uncertainties with courage and hope?

Visualize trust as the steady anchor, grounding you amidst life's storms, assuring you that, no matter the uncertainties, God's guidance remains a constant, unwavering force.

Let the sacred exploration of trusting God, serve as a vessel, carrying profound questions that invite introspection and contemplation into the very heart of trust amidst life's uncertainties.

Consider the uncertainties that currently inhabit your life.

How does the concept of trust influence your response to these unknowns?

Image trust not as a distant ideal but as a dynamic force, shaping your reactions and decisions in the face of life's unpredictable nature.

Reflect on the times when trust felt tested.

What anchors your trust in God during moments of doubt or confusion?

Start to envision trust as a resilient thread, woven through the fabric of your faith, holding steadfast even in life's uncertainties.

Contemplate the role of trust in shaping your relationship with God.

How does trust deepen the intimacy of your connection with the divine?

Picture trust as a bridge, spanning the gap between the known and the unknown, forging a pathway for a more profound communion with God.

Imagine the impact of trust on your perspective toward adversity.

How does a foundation of trust in God transform challenges from obstacles into opportunities for spiritual growth?

Let trust become a lens, reframing your outlook on uncertainties, turning them into stepping stones on your journey of faith.

Consider the narrative of your life.

How has trust in God influenced the unfolding chapters, especially in times of uncertainty?

Envision trust as a storyteller, weaving a narrative that transcends the immediate challenges, casting a vision of a purposeful journey guided by divine assurance.

Let these questions be companions, prompting you to delve into the depths of your trust in God.

In the dialogue with uncertainty, questions become lanterns, illuminating the path toward a more profound understanding of trust— a journey that unfolds with each contemplative step.

In the tapestry of my life, let me share an intimate testimony of the transformative power of trust in the Divine amidst life's unpredictable twists.

In moments of uncertainty, I found myself standing at the crossroads of fear and faith.

The unknown loomed like a formidable giant, casting shadows on the path ahead.

It was in these moments that the practice of trusting God became not just a spiritual concept but a lifeline, a beacon of hope that illuminated the darkness.

One of the defining moments of my story unfolds in a season of profound doubt.

The future seemed like an unwritten script, and the uncertainties were like uncharted territories.

Yet, it was precisely in this uncertainty that the whispers of Divine guidance became more pronounced.

Trust became the compass that guided each step, transforming the uncertainty into a sacred journey of discovery.

As life presented its share of challenges, trust in God emerged as a resilient force.

It was not a passive surrender but an active choice to anchor my spirit in the belief that, even amidst uncertainty, God's guidance is a sure and unwavering presence.

This trust became a sanctuary—a place of solace and strength amid life's storms.

Reflecting on my story, I see trust as a golden thread intricately woven through the chapters of adversity and triumph.

It was the balm that soothed wounds, the steady heartbeat that echoed through moments of joy and sorrow alike.

Trusting God was not just a response to uncertainty but a dynamic, transformative posture that shaped the narrative of my life.

As I share this personal story, I envision it not as an isolated testimony but as an invitation—an invitation to explore the profound dimensions of trust in your own narrative.

In the dance with uncertainty, may my words inspire a resonance with your own story, a reminder that trust in God is not merely a concept but a lived experience that can infuse purpose and resilience into the very fabric of your existence.

In the tapestry of your life, uncertainties may look like uncharted territories, but within the practice of trusting God lies the promise of divine guidance.

Picture yourself standing at the crossroads of fear and faith.

How might trust become your compass, directing your steps toward a future bathed in the glow of Divine assurance?

Consider your own moments of uncertainty.

Visualize trust not as a distant ideal but as a dynamic force, ready to shape your reactions and decisions.

Imagine trust becoming a resilient thread, intricately woven into the fabric of your faith, holding steadfast even amidst the storms of life.

Reflect on the challenges that dot your life's landscape.

How might the practice of trusting God transform these challenges into opportunities for spiritual growth?

Envision yourself not merely as a passive recipient of divine guidance but as an active co-creator of your destiny, anchored in the certainty that God's guidance is a sure and unwavering presence.

In the realm of your relationships, contemplate the impact of trust on the connections you foster.

How might trust become a bridge, forging deeper connections with others?

Envision your relationships bathed in the warmth of understanding and support, mirroring the divine trust that underlies your own journey.

You are not alone in your uncertainties. With each word, feel the encouragement to embrace trust as a transformative stance—a choice that shapes your story, turning uncertainties into opportunities for divine guidance and profound spiritual awakening.

Picture this moment as a sacred pause—a space for reflection on the trust that has unfolded within these pages.

The uncertainties you've faced, and the challenges you've conquered, are all underscored by the resounding heartbeat of trust in God.

As you turn the page, envision the wisdom gained from this chapter becoming the foundation for the spiritual connections awaiting you.

In the dance with uncertainty, trust becomes a melody, echoing through the corridors of your spirit.

As you step into "Spiritual Connections," imagine these connections not merely as relationships with others but as threads that weave a tapestry of shared faith and understanding.

Your journey, enriched by trust, now extends to the realm of communal spirituality.

Consider the relationships in your life.

As we transition, see them not in isolation but as opportunities for spiritual connections that deepen your understanding of God's love.

Picture yourself as a part of a vibrant community, where trust and shared faith become the bonds that strengthen connections, fostering an environment where everyone is uplifted.

In the upcoming chapter, "Spiritual Connections," imagine the practice of trusting God in shaping your interactions with others.

As you form bonds grounded in mutual trust, see how the collective spirituality becomes a force that transcends individual experiences.

You are not just a reader; you are an active participant in a narrative of shared faith, where spiritual connections blossom and flourish.

Feel the anticipation for the spiritual connections awaiting you.

It's not just the turning of a page; it's an invitation to delve deeper into the richness of shared faith and understanding.

As you step into "Spiritual Connections," let the trust cultivated in the previous chapter become the cornerstone for a community where hearts are intertwined, and the collective spirit is elevated by the bonds of shared spirituality.

Spiritual Connections

'And let us consider one another to provoke unto love and to good works: Not forsaking the assembling of ourselves together, as the manner of some is, but exhorting one another: and so much the more, as ye see the day approaching."
— Hebrews 10:24-25

WITHIN THE SANCTUARY OF SHARED BELIEFS, imagine your presence not as mere attendance but as a catalyst for the collective spirit.

Image yourself standing among fellow believers, a community united by the bonds of faith.

In these paragraphs, feel the warmth of shared spirituality enveloping you, fostering a sense of belonging that transcends individual experiences.

Consider the moments of communal worship and fellowship.

Envision your interactions not as isolated events but as opportunities to strengthen the tapestry of relationships within your faith community.

Picture the exchange of words and gestures as threads that weave a narrative of shared understanding and mutual support, creating connections that endure beyond the confines of a physical gathering.

In the realm of spiritual connections, imagine your role not just as a recipient of support but as a source of encouragement for others.

Envision your words and actions resonating within the hearts of your fellow believers, fostering an environment where everyone is uplifted.

As you engage in conversations and share moments of prayer, recognize the power you hold to contribute to the vibrancy of your faith community.

Picture the challenges faced by your faith community.

Whether it be times of adversity or moments of celebration, see yourself as an integral part of the collective response.

Sense the strength that comes from standing together, united in faith and mutual support.

Envision your faith community as a resilient tapestry, each thread contributing to the overall strength and endurance of the whole.

Let God's Word be like a mirror reflecting your vital role within the community.

See your presence as a divine appointment, a purposeful thread in the intricate weaving of relationships.

With each word, sense the profound impact you have in strengthening the communal bonds of faith, making your journey not just individual but an integral part of the vibrant tapestry of spiritual connections within your faith community.

In the ethereal dance of faith, envision your spirit reaching out to connect with others, forming a Divine Connection.

See your spiritual essence intertwining with the collective spirit of your faith community, fostering a tapestry of shared devotion, and understanding.

Envision the moments of communal worship as an intimate conversation between spirits.

In the hallowed spaces of prayer and praise, feel the resonance of your spirit harmonizing with those around you.

Sense the unity that arises when individual spirits converge in a collective dance of devotion, each one contributing to the spiritual symphony.

Envision your interactions within the faith community as encounters of spirit to spirit.

As you engage with fellow believers, recognize the divine spark within each soul.

Picture your words and actions as bridges, allowing the spirits to connect and communicate in the shared language of faith.

In these moments, understand that the strength of relationships lies not only in the physical interactions but in the spiritual exchanges that transcend the material realm.

Reflect on the challenges faced by your spiritual family.

In times of adversity, see your spirit as a source of solace and support.

Picture your prayers and intentions weaving a tapestry of spiritual fortitude, where each spirit contributes to the collective resilience.

Sense the interconnectedness of spirits, creating a communal sanctuary of strength and endurance.

Imagine your spiritual role extending beyond the confines of formal gatherings.

Envisage your spirit as a constant presence, weaving connections through the threads of shared experiences, joys, and sorrows.

Picture the relationships you cultivate as spiritual alliances, where the intertwining of spirits goes beyond the surface, forging a deeper connection in the realms unseen.

Envision your spirit as an active participant in the ongoing dance of connection, recognizing the sacred bonds formed when spirits converge in shared devotion.

With each word, feel the invitation to deepen your spiritual connections, fostering an environment where spirits unite and relationships flourish in the sacred dance of faith.

Embark on a profound exploration of spiritual connections.

Engage with the essence of spiritual connections through introspective questions, inviting your spirit to ponder and resonate with the collective spirit of your faith community.

The Dance of Souls

As you reflect on the communal worship within your faith community, envision the dance of souls. How does your spirit contribute to the collective symphony of devotion? Picture the intertwining of spirits in those moments of prayer and praise and consider the unique melody that your spirit adds to the spiritual dance.

Spirit-to-Spirit Exchanges

Consider your interactions within the faith community as exchanges of spirit to spirit. How does your spirit connect with others in the shared language of faith? Reflect on the depth of these spiritual encounters, recognizing that the strength of relationships lies not only in physical interactions but in the profound exchanges that occur at the spiritual level.

Resilient Spirits in Adversity

In times of adversity, contemplate the resilience of spirits within your spiritual family. How does your spirit serve as a source of solace and support? Visualize your prayers and intentions weaving a tapestry of spiritual fortitude, where each spirit contributes to the collective strength. Explore the interconnectedness of spirits, creating a communal sanctuary of endurance.

The Unseen Threads of Spiritual Alliances

Envision your spiritual role extending beyond formal gatherings. Picture your spirit as a constant presence, weaving connections through the unseen threads of shared experiences. How do these spiritual alliances deepen your connections? Explore the profound intertwining of spirits that goes beyond surface-level interactions, forging a deeper and enduring bond.

A Sanctuary for Spirit Unions

Reflect on the significance of your spirit actively participating in the ongoing dance of connection. Consider how your spiritual engagement fosters an environment where spirits unite, and relationships flourish in the sacred dance of faith.

Let spirit-to-spirit questions guide you into a contemplative exploration of the profound connections within your faith community.

Feel the resonance of your spirit as it intertwines with the collective spirit, forging bonds that transcend the physical and dive deep into the spiritual realms of shared faith.

In the sanctity of our communal worship, I recall a particular moment of vulnerability when my spirit resonated deeply with those around me.

During a period of personal struggle, the collective spirit of our faith community became a refuge, offering solace beyond words.

In the shared silence of prayer and the unity of our hearts, I realized the profound strength that emerges when individual spirits converge in a collective symphony of devotion.

Engaging in spirit-to-spirit exchanges within our faith community has been a journey of discovery.

I remember a conversation where our spirits connected on a level deeper than mere words.

It was in that exchange that I recognized the power of spiritual communication, realizing that relationships are not only forged through shared experiences but also through the unseen currents of faith that bind our spirits together.

In the face of adversity, the resilience of our collective spirits became evident.

A personal challenge within my life mirrored the challenges faced by our faith community.

As we joined hands in prayer and mutual support, I witnessed the strength that arises when spirits unite.

This shared spiritual fortitude not only sustained me personally but also fortified the bonds within our faith family.

The spiritual alliances formed beyond our formal gatherings have been particularly impactful.

I recall instances where shared experiences became threads, weaving connections that transcended the boundaries of time and space.

These alliances have cultivated an enduring sense of community, transforming the faith community into a tapestry of spiritual connections that extend far beyond the physical confines of our gatherings.

Reflecting on these personal stories, I recognize that my spirit is an integral part of the ongoing dance of connection within our faith community.

Each encounter, shared prayer, and moment of vulnerability has contributed to the vibrant tapestry of spiritual connections.

As I continue to navigate the chapters of "Spiritual Connections," I am reminded that my story is interwoven with those around me, creating a narrative of shared faith that strengthens the bonds within our spiritual family.

Envision yourself as a vital thread intricately woven into the fabric of collective faith.

As these words unfold, feel the resonance of your spirit actively participating in the transformative dance of connection within your faith community.

Imagine the moments of communal worship as personal encounters with the Divine.

Envision your spirit harmonizing with fellow believers, creating a symphony of shared devotion.

Understand that your presence is not incidental but an essential note in the melody of collective spirituality, contributing to the richness of the faith community.

Consider your interactions within the faith community as opportunities for profound connections.

Picture your spirit engaging in meaningful exchanges, bridging the gap between individual experiences and shared faith.

Recognize the significance of your contributions, as your words and actions become threads that weave a fabric of compassion and understanding among fellow believers.

Reflect on the challenges faced by your spiritual family.

As you navigate times of adversity, see your spirit as a source of strength and support.

Envision your prayers and intentions intermingling with the collective prayers of the community, creating a tapestry of resilience.

In these moments, acknowledge the profound impact your spirit has on fortifying the communal bonds of faith.

Imagine your spiritual role extending beyond the confines of formal gatherings.

Envisage yourself as a constant presence, weaving connections through shared experiences, joys, and sorrows.

Picture the relationships you cultivate becoming spiritual alliances, where the intertwining of spirits fosters a deeper connection in the realms unseen.

See your engagement not as a mere routine but as a sacred responsibility, recognizing the transformative power of your contributions.

With each word, feel the invitation to actively participate in the nurturing of spiritual connections, fostering an environment where your spirit unites with others, and relationships flourish in the sacred dance of faith.

As we conclude the illuminating chapter of "Spiritual Connections: Strengthening Relationships," let these closing paragraphs be a moment of reflection and anticipation.

This chapter has been a journey of shared faith, connecting spirits within the tapestry of your spiritual community.

Now, as we transition into the next chapter, "Mindful Spirituality," let the anticipation for what lies ahead fill your spirit.

Picture this upcoming chapter not just as a shift in focus but as a continuation of the spiritual journey.

"Mindful Spirituality" invites you to explore the depths of your spiritual practices and connections with heightened awareness and intention.

Consider how mindful spirituality can deepen your engagement within your faith community.

Envision your spirit becoming attuned to the present moment, fostering a deeper connection with the divine and those around you.

As you step into this new chapter, embrace the transformative power of mindfulness in shaping your spiritual experiences and relationships.

Reflect on the lessons learned in the previous chapter and carry them forward into the exploration of mindful spirituality.

Picture the tapestry of connections formed in the previous chapter becoming a foundation for the mindfulness that will unfold.

Let the wisdom gained from strengthening relationships guide your practice of mindful spirituality.

Imagine your spirit becoming more attuned, more present, and more connected.

Each word within the upcoming chapter is an invitation to explore the depths of mindfulness in your spiritual journey.

With gratitude for the connections forged, step into the next chapter, ready to embrace the transformative potential of "Mindful Spirituality" within the sanctuary of your faith community.

CHAPTER SEVEN

Mindful Spirituality

Finally, brethren, whatsoever things are true, whatsoever things are honest, whatsoever things are just, whatsoever things are pure, whatsoever things are lovely, whatsoever things are of good report; if there be any virtue, and if there be any praise, think on these things."
– Philippians 4:8

IN THE SACRED JOURNEY OF MINDFUL SPIRITUALITY, you find yourself standing at the intersection of your thoughts and the divine grace of God.

As you embark on this path of mental wellness, envision your mind as a garden ready for cultivation, awaiting the gentle touch of God's grace to nurture its flourishing.

Picture the canvas of your thoughts becoming a sacred space where mindfulness takes root.

Imagine God's grace gently descending like rain, nurturing the seeds of peace, joy, and clarity within your mind.

Feel the transformative power of mindfulness as it intertwines with the divine grace, creating a harmonious landscape within the sanctuary of your thoughts.

Consider your moments of meditation and reflection as an intimate dialogue with the divine.

Envision your mind becoming a receptive vessel, open to the whispers of God's guidance.

Picture the alignment of your thoughts with God's truth, fostering a mental wellness that transcends the temporal challenges.

In these moments, recognize the profound connection between mindful spirituality and the renewing grace of God.

Reflect on the storms of life and the chaos that may swirl within your mind.

Envision God's grace as a calming force, gently settling the waves of anxiety and uncertainty.

See the serenity that descends upon your thoughts when anchored in the mindfulness of God's presence.

Experience the assurance that mental wellness is not just a personal endeavor but a divine partnership.

Imagine the daily practice of mindfulness as a sacred rhythm, a dance between your consciousness and God's grace.

Envision your thoughts becoming attuned to the present moment, each breath a reminder of the Divine presence.

Picture the stillness within, a sanctuary where God's grace dwells, nurturing the roots of mental wellness.

In these moments of mindful spirituality, understand that your consciousness is intertwined with the eternal grace of God.

Envision your journey not merely as a quest for mental wellness but as a sacred pilgrimage, where God's grace guides every mindful step, fostering a flourishing garden of peace and serenity within the landscape of your thoughts.

In the realm of mindful spirituality, you stand as a seeker of tranquility and mental well-being, ready to embrace the transformative power of God's grace.

As you delve deeper into this sacred practice, envision your mind as a vessel, open to the gentle infusion of Divine presence.

Allow the synergy between your conscious awareness and God's grace to weave a tapestry of serenity within the intricate landscape of your thoughts.

Picture the daily rhythm of your life as a symphony, each note harmonizing with the grace of God.

Envision moments of mindfulness as a sacred pause in this symphony, a time when the divine melody resonates within the chambers of your mind.

Just feel the cadence of your breath aligning with the eternal heartbeat of God's grace, nurturing a mental wellness that transcends the transient melodies of life.

Consider the challenges that life presents and the inevitable storms that may buffet your mind.

Envision God's grace as an anchor, grounding you amidst the tumultuous waves of stress and uncertainty.

Picture mindfulness practice as a lifeline, connecting you to the unwavering source of divine peace.

In these moments, understand that mental wellness is not about avoiding storms but finding solace in the unchanging grace of God amid them.

Imagine the process of cultivating mindfulness as a sacred garden, with each intentional breath and reflective thought acting as seeds of spiritual growth.

See God's grace as the nurturing sunlight, providing the energy needed for these seeds to blossom into thoughts of love, kindness, and gratitude.

Imagine the richness of the soil within your mind, now fertile with the grace-driven potential for enduring mental wellness.

Reflect on the interconnectedness between your spiritual journey and the grace of God.

Envision mindfulness not as a solitary pursuit but as a dance with the Divine, each step guided by the grace that flows from a higher source.

Picture the synergy between your intentionality and God's benevolence, creating a sacred space within your mind where mental wellness becomes a manifestation of the Divine presence.

In these moments, recognize that the grace of God is not distant but an intimate companion in your mindful exploration.

Envision your conscious awareness as a vessel ready to receive the divine grace, and may the journey of mindful spirituality lead you to a profound and enduring mental wellness, guided and sustained by the unwavering grace of God.

In the sacred realm of mindful spirituality, let your consciousness be a canvas where the transformative questions of God's grace paint a portrait of mental well-being.

As you embark on this introspective journey, envision your mind as a sanctuary where these questions resonate, echoing through the corridors of your thoughts.

1. What does it mean to invite God's grace into your moments of mindfulness? Reflect on the essence of your practice. How can the intentional presence of God's grace elevate the quality of your mindful moments? Picture each breath becoming a sacred inhalation of divine tranquility, filling the canvas of your mind with hues of serenity.

2. How does the concept of divine grace reshape your understanding of mental wellness? Consider the relationship between grace and mental well-being. How does acknowledging the grace of God transform your perception of challenges and joys? Envision mental wellness not just as an individual endeavor but as a collaborative dance with the divine.

3. In what ways can mindfulness serve as a bridge to connect with God's grace in your daily life? Contemplate the practical integration of mindfulness and divine grace. Picture your daily routines becoming opportunities for connection. How can each moment, from routine tasks to profound experiences, be infused with mindful awareness, fostering a continuous communion with God's grace?

4. How might the storms within your mind find solace in the calming embrace of God's grace? Explore the metaphor of storms as challenges within your mind. How does the awareness of God's grace act as a stabilizing force amid these storms? Envision a mental landscape where the turbulence of thoughts finds stillness in the abiding presence of divine tranquility.

5. Can the practice of mindful spirituality be a conduit for a deeper understanding of God's grace? Consider the reciprocity between mindfulness and divine understanding. How does your practice deepen your comprehension of God's grace? Picture each moment of mindfulness as a portal to a profound connection with the divine, nurturing mental wellness that extends beyond the surface of conscious thought.

Let these questions be guiding lights, illuminating the path toward a deeper understanding of the intertwining dance between your conscious awareness, the practice of mindfulness, and the enriching grace of God.

I would like to share a personal journey where the intertwining forces of mindfulness and divine grace became the guiding light through the labyrinth of my mental landscape.

In the quiet moments of contemplation, I recall a time when the storms of life brewed tumultuously within my mind.

Anxiety and uncertainty cast shadows, threatening to obscure the clarity I sought.

It was then that I embarked on a mindful journey, a conscious effort to invite God's grace into the tempest of my thoughts.

As I delved into the practice, each breath became a prayer, and with time, the storms began to settle, revealing the serenity that lies beneath the surface.

In the tapestry of my daily routine, mindfulness became more than a practice; it became a sacred ritual of connection with the Divine.

I discovered that God's grace wasn't confined to specific moments of prayer but could permeate every facet of my existence.

From the mundane to the profound, mindfulness became a thread weaving through the fabric of my thoughts, infusing each moment with the transformative power of grace.

There were instances when life presented unexpected challenges, and the demands of the external world seemed overwhelming.

In these moments, the practice of mindful spirituality emerged as a sanctuary.

God's grace became the anchor, grounding me amidst the chaos.

I found solace in the awareness that, even amid uncertainty, I could navigate the currents of life with a steady heart, guided by the grace that dwelled within.

The garden of my thoughts, once neglected, began to flourish with the intentional cultivation of mindfulness.

Like a diligent gardener, I sowed seeds of gratitude, compassion, and love.

With each breath, I watered these seeds, and with God's grace as sunlight, they sprouted into a lush landscape of mental wellness.

The practice of mindfulness wasn't just a routine but a sacred dance where I partnered with the divine to nurture the flourishing garden within.

Reflecting on this journey, I've come to understand that mindful spirituality is not a destination but a continuous exploration.

It's a journey where God's grace and my conscious awareness intertwine, creating a tapestry of mental well-being.

As I share these paragraphs, I hope they serve as a testament to the transformative potential that lies within the marriage of mindful spirituality and God's grace, offering a guiding light for those who tread a similar path.

Now envision yourself not just as a spectator but as an active participant in a profound journey of self-discovery and spiritual awakening.

Let's explore the transformative landscape of your mental well-being.

Your Conscious Breath

As you embark on the pages ahead, consider the simple yet profound act of conscious breathing. Imagine each inhalation as an opportunity to invite the grace of God into the depths of your being. Picture the exhalation as a release, letting go of the burdens that may weigh on your mind. In this practice, discover the power of your breath as a conduit for divine presence.

Your Mindful Sanctuary

Envision your mind as a sanctuary, a sacred space where the clutter of daily life can be gently set aside. As you read these words, let the awareness blossom that, in the quiet moments of mindful spirituality, you hold the key to unlock the door to this inner sanctuary. Allow your consciousness to be a welcomed guest, invited to dwell in the serenity that unfolds within the embrace of God's grace.

Your Mental Garden

Reflect on the landscape of your thoughts. Picture your mind as a garden waiting to be nurtured. With each sentence, consider how the practice of mindfulness becomes the gentle rain, and God's grace the nourishing sunlight. Envision the seeds of positive thoughts and loving intentions sprouting, creating a lush mental garden that blossoms under the tender care of your conscious awareness and divine grace.

Your Dance with the Divine

Envision your spirituality not as a distant concept but as a dance with the divine. As you read on, feel the rhythm of this dance, the ebb and flow of your conscious connection with God's grace. See each word as a step, leading you closer to a harmonious partnership where mindful awareness and divine presence intertwine in a sacred choreography that nurtures your mental well-being.

Your Invitation to Transformation

As these paragraphs unfold, recognize that you are not merely a passive reader but an active participant in the transformational narrative of mindful spirituality. Feel the invitation extended to you—an invitation to explore, question, and embrace the potential for mental wellness through the grace of God. Picture each word as a stepping stone, guiding you towards the realization that, within the tapestry of these pages, your own journey of spiritual and mental transformation awaits.

In the sacred tapestry of your mindful journey, each moment has been a brushstroke, painting the canvas of your consciousness with the hues of divine grace.

As you stand at the threshold of the eighth chapter, "Wisdom Seeking," envision the upcoming pages as a portal to profound insights, beckoning you to explore the boundless realms where mindfulness and divine wisdom intertwine.

In the preceding chapters, you've cultivated a garden of mental well-being, nourished by the gentle rain of mindful awareness and the warm sunlight of God's grace.

Now, as you transition into the chapter of "Wisdom Seeking," see this garden expanding into a vast landscape where each bloom is a revelation, and every step forward is a journey into the depths of spiritual understanding.

Consider the journey inward not as a mere exploration but as a pilgrimage to the very essence of your soul.

Imagine stepping onto the sacred path that winds through the corridors of your consciousness.

Let mindfulness be your guiding lantern, illuminating the way as you seek the timeless wisdom that resides within the sanctum of your being.

As you embark on the pages ahead, picture the words becoming whispers of divine insight, resonating with the deepest chambers of your heart.

See each sentence as a guidepost, leading you further into the realms where the grace of God and the pursuit of wisdom merge in a dance of profound understanding.

In this transition, recognize that wisdom is not a distant destination but a companion, ever-present in the mindful awareness of each moment.

Consider the integration of mindfulness and wisdom not as a juxtaposition but as a seamless fusion.

Envision your consciousness as a vessel, ready to receive the sacred elixir that wisdom offers.

Feel the currents of spiritual enlightenment flowing through these pages, carrying you into the heart of "Wisdom Seeking."

CHAPTER EIGHT

Wisdom Seeking

"Thy word is a lamp unto my feet, and a light unto my path."
— Psalm 119:105

AS WE STEP INTO THIS CHAPTER, LET THE SPIRIT'S whisper be your compass, steering you through the complexities of life's questions and uncertainties.

Picture each word as a revelation, an invitation to delve deeper into the wellspring of divine knowledge.

In this chapter, the Holy Spirit becomes your gentle guide, navigating the sacred corridors of wisdom and offering clarity in the embrace of God's counsel.

May you find solace in the Spirit's presence, a presence that transcends time and space, resonating within the very fabric of your being.

As you read, allow the Spirit's whisper to cultivate a sense of profound connection with the eternal truths that illuminate the path to spiritual understanding.

May the insights gained in these pages become a beacon, guiding you through the sacred journey of wisdom-seeking and leading you to the embrace of God's eternal counsel.

The Gentle Whisper of Inquiry

Feel the gentle whisper of inquiry within your spirit. Let the rustle of the pages lead you to turn your heart toward God. Sense the guiding presence of the Holy Spirit, gently nudging you toward the profound insights embedded in the counsel of God.

The Radiant Illumination

Picture the words on these pages as rays of Divine light, penetrating the depths of your consciousness. As you read, envision the Holy Spirit illuminating the corridors of your understanding. Each paragraph becomes a beacon, guiding you to clarity and understanding in alignment with the divine counsel. Feel the warmth of the Spirit's guidance as you navigate through the complexities of the spiritual journey.

The Eternal Conversation

Envision the narrative as an eternal conversation facilitated by the Holy Spirit. Feel the Spirit's resonance with the timeless wisdom that transcends the boundaries of human comprehension. Picture the pages as a sacred space where the Spirit engages in a dialogue with your seeking soul, responding to your questions with the profound wisdom that emanates from God's counsel.

The Sanctified Contemplation

Consider your mind as a sanctified space for contemplation, a sacred temple where the Holy Spirit finds resonance. Allow the Spirit to expand the sanctuary within, creating room for divine thoughts and insights to take root. Envision the stillness of this sacred space, where the clarity of God's counsel echoes through the gentle prompting of the Holy Spirit.

The Unveiling of Divine Patterns

Perceive the unfolding of divine patterns through the lens of the Holy Spirit. Envision the tapestry of spiritual understanding unfurling before your spiritual eyes, guided by the hand of the Holy Spirit. In these moments, feel the Spirit's presence shaping the narrative of divine clarity in your journey of wisdom-seeking.

The Holy Spirit's Beckoning

Feel the gentle beckoning of the Holy Spirit. Envision the Spirit as a guiding presence, extending an invitation to explore the depths of divine wisdom. Sense the Spirit's call, drawing you closer to the wellspring of insight and understanding that flows from the eternal counsel of God.

The Radiance of Divine Illumination

Imagine the words on these pages as streams of divine illumination, flowing from the Holy Spirit's eternal source. Feel the radiant light of wisdom piercing through the shadows of uncertainty. Each flash of light becomes a conduit of the Spirit's clarity, casting away the darkness and revealing the brilliance of God's counsel in the sacred journey of wisdom-seeking.

The Continuing Conversation

Picture the pages as a space where questions are met with answers, and where the divine guidance of the Spirit shapes the contours of your understanding. In this sacred dialogue, let the Spirit's voice resonate as a timeless companion on your quest for clarity.

The Sanctified Sanctuary of Reflection

Consider your mind as a sanctified sanctuary, a dwelling place for the Holy Spirit's reflections. Let the Spirit expand this sacred space, creating room for contemplation and deep communion. Envision the stillness within, where the Spirit's voice echoes like a sacred hymn, bringing peace and understanding as you reflect on the timeless wisdom of God's counsel.

The Unfolding Tapestry of Divine Insight

Envision the Holy Spirit weaving an unfolding tapestry of divine insight. Picture each action as a thread carefully placed by the Spirit's hand, contributing to the intricate design of God's wisdom. In this tapestry, feel the Spirit's artistry at work, creating a masterpiece of understanding that tells a story of clarity, purpose, and divine counsel.

The Inquiry of Spiritual Depth

Let the Holy Spirit prompt you with questions that resonate in the depths of your soul. Ask yourself, what truths lie beneath the surface of your understanding? What wellsprings of wisdom await your discovery as you tread the path of spiritual depth and clarity in the embrace of God's counsel?

The Quest for Personal Revelation

Allow the Holy Spirit to guide your introspection. What personal revelations does God's counsel hold for you in this moment? In the tapestry of your unique journey, what threads of insight are waiting to be woven into the fabric of your understanding? Consider these questions as keys to unlocking the doors of revelation on your quest for clarity.

The Reflection on Divine Purpose

Guided by the questions whispered by the Holy Spirit. What is the divine purpose that beckons you forward? How does the counsel of God shape your understanding of purpose and clarity in the grand tapestry of existence? Let the Spirit's questions lead you to a deeper contemplation of the purpose that aligns with the eternal wisdom of God.

The Inquiry into Personal Growth

In the gentle rustle of the Spirit's voice, reflect upon your journey of personal growth. What lessons and insights does the counsel of God offer for your growth and transformation? How can the clarity sought in this chapter become a catalyst for your spiritual evolution? Embrace these questions as invitations to explore the profound depths of your own spiritual maturation.

The Examination of Spiritual Connection

Dive into the Spirit's questions that probe the essence of spiritual connection. How does your connection with the Divine influence your pursuit of clarity? What sacred threads bind you to the eternal truths embedded in God's counsel? Allow these questions to unravel the intricacies of your spiritual connection, guiding you to a deeper understanding in the chapters that unfold.

May these questions, voiced by the Holy Spirit, serve as companions on your journey as you seek to hear God's Counsel." Let them be lanterns that illuminate the path of introspection, leading you to profound insights and a richer connection with the timeless wisdom that awaits in the embrace of Divine counsel.

The Unveiling of Personal Journey

Allow me to share a personal story, a glimpse into the pages of my journey of wisdom-seeking and clarity in God's counsel. There was a time when uncertainty cast its shadows over my path, and questions echoed within the chambers of my soul. In the tapestry of my existence, each thread seemed disconnected, yet the Holy Spirit guided me with gentle whispers, leading me toward the profound insights waiting to be discovered.

Navigating the Wilderness of Doubt

Picture a season in my life when the wilderness of doubt seemed vast and daunting. The questions that echoed in my heart were met with a patient silence as if God Himself was waiting for the perfect moment to unveil the clarity that would dispel the shadows. Through prayer and contemplation, I learned that sometimes the journey to understanding requires patience, trust, and an unwavering belief in the guidance of the Holy Spirit.

The Revelation Amidst Challenges

Amid life's challenges, I experienced a revelation that transformed the way I perceived God's counsel. It was as if a veil had been lifted, and I could see the divine patterns woven into the fabric of my trials. The clarity I sought became intertwined with the lessons learned through hardship, revealing a deeper understanding of God's wisdom and purpose in every twist and turn.

The Tapestry of Redemption

Let me share a time when redemption played a central role. In moments of personal struggle and failure, the Holy Spirit guided me toward the redemptive threads woven into the narrative of my life. Through God's counsel, I discovered that even the darkest threads could be transformed into hues of grace, creating a tapestry that spoke of forgiveness, restoration, and the enduring love of a compassionate Creator.

The Joyful Harmony of Surrender

A pivotal moment in my wisdom-seeking journey was marked by the sweet surrender of my will to God's guidance. It was in the act of relinquishing control that I found an unparalleled clarity, like a melody orchestrated by the Holy Spirit. In this surrender, I discovered that true wisdom is often found in aligning my desires with the divine will, creating a harmonious symphony that resonates with the eternal truths woven into God's counsel.

These glimpses into my personal journey are shared with the hope that they resonate with your own quest for wisdom and clarity in the embrace of God's counsel. May these stories serve as testimonies to the transformative power of divine guidance in our lives.

A Beacon in the Dark

In the tapestry of my life, there was a season when the path ahead seemed shrouded in darkness. Questions about purpose and direction loomed large, casting shadows on my journey. It was during this time of uncertainty that the Holy Spirit became a beacon, gently guiding me toward the profound clarity found in God's counsel. Each step, though hesitant, became a testimony to the Spirit's unwavering presence, illuminating the way with a light that transcended the temporal gloom.

Lessons in Patience

One of the most transformative times in my wisdom-seeking journey unfolded through lessons of patience. The Holy Spirit, like a masterful teacher, led me through a curriculum of waiting and trust. In the waiting, I discovered that clarity often arrives at the perfect intersection of divine timing and surrendered patience. The pages of my story echoed the virtues of perseverance, and in the end, I found that the wisdom gained through patient endurance was a treasure beyond measure.

The Healing Power of Forgiveness

There was a season marked by the need for forgiveness – both of others and, perhaps more challenging, of myself. The Holy Spirit, in His gentle counsel, guided me toward the liberating act of letting go. Through the pages of forgiveness, I experienced a profound clarity that transcended the scars of past mistakes. It was a healing balm, and the narrative of my life spoke of redemption and the transformative power of God's counsel in the realm of relationships.

Divine Synchronicities

In the rhythm of my existence, there were moments when divine synchronicities orchestrated by the Holy Spirit became apparent. Instances where seemingly unrelated events converged to reveal a tapestry of purpose and meaning. Through these synchronicities, I understood that God's counsel is not confined to the pages of scripture alone but is intricately woven into the fabric of our daily lives. It was a time when the ordinary became extraordinary and the mundane spoke of the divine presence orchestrating every detail.

Joy in Surrender

The most joyous season in my wisdom-seeking journey were those where surrender became a way of life. Surrendering my plans, my fears, and my desires to the will of God ushered in a clarity that surpassed my understanding. The Holy Spirit, in His gentle persuasion, taught me that true wisdom lies in yielding to the divine purpose. In the surrender, I found a joy that transcended circumstances, and the pages of my life resonated with a melody of contentment orchestrated by the divine hand.

May you find resonance with the transformative power of divine guidance in the unique story of your life.

Embrace the Quest for Understanding

You, dear seeker, are on a quest for understanding that transcends the boundaries of the mundane. Embrace the questions that stir within your heart, for they are the catalysts propelling you toward the radiant clarity found in the counsel of God. Allow the whispers of the Holy Spirit to guide you through the labyrinth of uncertainty, leading you to profound insights that await your discovery.

You Are Woven into Divine Tapestry

Picture yourself as a thread intricately woven into the divine tapestry of existence. Know that the Holy Spirit, like a master weaver, is crafting a narrative that speaks of purpose, redemption, and the eternal truths embedded in God's counsel. You are an integral part of this grand design.

Find Strength in Patience

In the moments of waiting, find strength, dear reader. Patience is not a passive act but a courageous stance that allows the wisdom of God to unfold in its perfect time. The Holy Spirit is your companion in the waiting, teaching you the art of endurance and guiding you toward the clarity that blossoms when the moment is ripe. Trust the process, for with patience, profound insights take root.

Celebrate the Symphony of Surrender

Imagine your life as a symphony, and surrender is the melody that harmonizes with the divine score. Embrace the joy found in yielding to the will of God, for in surrender, you open yourself to the orchestrations of the Holy Spirit. As you read, let these words resonate within you, encouraging you to dance to the rhythm of Divine guidance, finding joy in the surrender that leads to clarity.

Your Story Unfolds in Divine Synchronicity

Recognize the divine synchronicities in your life. Your story is not a haphazard collection of events, but a tapestry woven with purpose and meaning. The Holy Spirit is the divine choreographer, orchestrating moments that converge to reveal the profound clarity of God's counsel.

Embrace the beauty of these synchronicities and find inspiration in the realization that your life unfolds in perfect harmony with the divine plan.

A Blessing of Divine Presence

May the awareness of the Divine Presence accompany you like a fragrant perfume, a lingering reminder that God's counsel is not confined to these pages but is a continuous flow, an eternal river of wisdom ready to nourish your spirit. Be assured that, in every step, the Holy Spirit walks beside you, a faithful guide in your quest for understanding.

The Gentle Assurance of Guidance

Let the Holy Spirit assure you of His unwavering guidance. Like a gentle hand on your shoulder, the Spirit beckons you to trust the unfolding narrative of your life. As you seek clarity, remember that the Spirit's guidance is not bound by time or circumstance. Allow this assurance to be a balm for your weary soul, a reminder that you are not alone in the pursuit of divine wisdom.

An Invitation to Reflection

The Holy Spirit extends an invitation to reflective communion. In the stillness, ponder the insights garnered, the questions stirred, and the divine moments encountered. Picture this reflection as a sacred conversation between your heart and the Spirit, a dialogue that transcends the written words and delves into the depths of your soul's yearning for wisdom.

The Blessing of Endurance

Embrace the blessing of endurance whispered by the Holy Spirit. Each step of your wisdom-seeking journey is an act of endurance, a testament to the resilience of your spirit. Through trials and triumphs, the Spirit encourages you to press on, knowing that the clarity sought is often found in the perseverance of the soul. May the endurance cultivated in these pages be a source of strength in the chapters yet to unfold.

A Parting Promise of Revelation

In the parting moments, let the Holy Spirit breathe a promise into your heart – a promise of ongoing revelation. Know that the pursuit of wisdom is not finite but a continual unveiling of divine mysteries. As you step away from these words, carry with you the anticipation of future revelations, for the Spirit, in His infinite wisdom, has more to share with you on this sacred journey of seeking clarity in the counsel of God.

Dear seeker, may the closing words spoken by the Holy Spirit linger as a sacred echo in your soul. May the insights gained in this chapter be seeds planted in the fertile soil of your spirit, ready to bloom into a garden of divine wisdom in the chapters yet to be written.

With a divine exhale, I usher you into the next sacred terrain, "Embracing Purpose Amidst the Unknown." Just as the Spirit has been your guide in seeking clarity, let His presence continue to be the compass that directs you toward the purpose woven into the intricate design of your journey.

"Embracing Purpose Amidst the Unknown." with faith, for it is in the dance of uncertainty that the purpose unfolds, and the Holy Spirit, your eternal guide, leads you toward the revelation of divine intentions in the chapter that awaits.

CHAPTER NINE

Embracing Purpose Amidst The Unknown

For I know the thoughts that I think toward you, saith the Lord, thoughts of peace, and not of evil, to give you an expected end."
– Jeremiah 29:11

BELOVED, KNOW THAT YOU ARE CRADLED IN THE arms of divine love. As you embark on the journey of embracing purpose amidst the unknown, feel the gentle embrace of the Holy Spirit guiding you, whispering wisdom, and unveiling the purpose that awaits in the dance of the unknown.

Beloved Seeker, Hear My Whisper

In the sacred chambers of your heart, I, the Holy Spirit, extend a gentle whisper. As you stand at the crossroads of the unknown, listen closely. There, in the hallowed silence, you will hear the rhythmic beats of purpose calling your name. Let not the vastness of uncertainty drown this sacred call; rather, let it guide you towards the purpose that awaits, intricately woven into the tapestry of your existence.

Illuminate the Shadows of Doubt

Fear not the shadows that dance in the unknown, for I am the light that pierces through the darkness. In the shadows of doubt and uncertainty, I illuminate the path before you. Allow the radiance of divine purpose to dispel the shadows that attempt to obscure your vision. With each step, trust that I am your constant companion, guiding you toward the purpose designed by the Creator's hands.

Your Purpose Unfolds in Divine Timing

As you navigate the uncharted waters of purpose, remember that I, the Holy Spirit, am the keeper of divine timing. Your purpose is not a destination to be hastily reached; rather, it is an exquisite unveiling orchestrated by the Creator. Embrace patience, dear traveler, for in the rhythm of divine timing, you will witness the purposeful symphony of your life unfolding in perfect harmony.

Courage Is Birthed in Your Spirit

The unknown may stir apprehension within you, but be assured, I am the cultivator of courage in your spirit. Every courageous step you take in the face of uncertainty resonates with the divine courage breathed into your being. Allow the courage within to be a beacon, lighting the way towards the purpose that beckons. You are not alone; I am the wind beneath your wings, lifting you to new heights.

In Every Choice, Purpose Resides

As you navigate the myriad choices presented by the unknown, recognize that purpose resides in the very fabric of each decision. I am the silent guide, nudging you towards choices that align with the grand tapestry of your purpose. Embrace the present, for it is in the now that purpose is nurtured. With each choice, you carve a path that leads you closer to the revelation of the divine purpose intricately woven into your existence.

A Blessing of Divine Presence

May the awareness of the Divine Presence accompany you like a fragrant perfume, a lingering reminder that God's counsel is not confined to these pages but is a continuous flow, an eternal river of wisdom ready to nourish your spirit. Be assured that, in every step, the Holy Spirit walks beside you, a faithful guide in your quest for understanding.

The Gentle Assurance of Guidance

In the closing moments, let the Holy Spirit assure you of His unwavering guidance. Like a gentle hand on your shoulder, the Spirit beckons you to trust the unfolding narrative of your life. As you seek clarity, remember that the Spirit's guidance is not bound by time or circumstance. Allow this assurance to be a balm for your weary soul, a reminder that you are not alone in the pursuit of divine wisdom.

An Invitation to Reflection

The Holy Spirit extends an invitation to reflective communion. In the stillness, ponder the insights garnered, the questions stirred, and the divine moments encountered. Picture this reflection as a sacred conversation between your heart and the Spirit, a dialogue that transcends the written words and delves into the depths of your soul's yearning for wisdom.

The Blessing of Endurance

Embrace the blessing of endurance whispered by the Holy Spirit. Each step of your wisdom-seeking journey is an act of endurance, a testament to the resilience of your spirit. Through trials and triumphs, the Spirit encourages you to press on, knowing that the clarity sought is often found in the perseverance of the soul. May the endurance cultivated in these pages be a source of strength in the chapters yet to unfold.

A Promise of Revelation

Let the Holy Spirit breathe a promise into your heart – a promise of ongoing revelation. Know that the pursuit of wisdom is not finite but a continual unveiling of divine mysteries. As you step away from these words, carry with you the anticipation of future revelations, for the Spirit, in His infinite wisdom, has more to share with you on this sacred journey of seeking clarity in the counsel of God.

Have You Listened to the Whispers of Your Soul?

In the quiet moments, have you allowed the whispers of your soul to rise above the clamor of the world? The Holy Spirit speaks through the gentle nudges within. Have you listened to the divine counsel echoing in the depths of your being, guiding you toward clarity and purpose?

Do You Embrace the Unknown with Faith?

As you navigate the uncharted territories of life, do you approach the unknown with faith as your compass? Have you considered that, in the uncertainty, there exists an opportunity to deepen your trust in the divine guidance of the Holy Spirit? Faith is the key that unlocks the door to profound insights and a purposeful journey.

Have You Explored the Shadows with Courage?

Amidst the shadows of doubt and fear, have you ventured forward with courage? The Holy Spirit is a beacon of courage within you. Have you allowed that inner light to pierce through the darkness, revealing the path of purpose that may be hidden in the corners of your uncertainties?

Do You Recognize Purpose in Everyday Choices?

In the tapestry of your daily life, have you recognized the threads of purpose woven into seemingly ordinary choices? The Holy Spirit guides you in each decision, no matter how small. Have you contemplated the significance of these choices in shaping the grand design of your purpose?

Are You Patiently Waiting for Divine Timing?

As you seek wisdom and clarity, are you willing to be patient and trust in divine timing? The Holy Spirit orchestrates the symphony of your life. Have you considered that, in the pauses and moments of waiting, there may be a divine revelation unfolding, shaping the purpose of your journey?

These questions are not meant to overwhelm but to invite introspection. Allow the Holy Spirit to illuminate the answers within your heart, guiding you on the sacred path of wisdom-seeking and purposeful living.

In Ages Past, I Whispered to Solomon

In the tapestry of ages past, there was a seeker of wisdom named Solomon. In the stillness of his heart, I, the Holy Spirit, whispered guidance, offering him clarity beyond measure. Solomon, with an open heart and a thirst for understanding, sought not earthly treasures but the profound wisdom that comes from God's counsel. Have you, too, considered the treasure trove of wisdom waiting for you in the divine whispers?

A Modern Pilgrim's Journey

Consider the modern pilgrim, much like yourself, navigating the complexities of life. In a world abuzz with noise, distractions, and uncertainties, the Holy Spirit remains a steadfast guide. Just as in ancient times, the Spirit's voice echoes in the corridors of your soul, offering timeless wisdom and clarity amidst the cacophony of the contemporary pilgrimage. Can you discern the echoes of the Holy Spirit in your journey?

Through Life's Storms, a Beacon of Hope

Picture a ship sailing through turbulent seas, buffeted by life's storms. In these tempestuous moments, the Holy Spirit is the unwavering compass, providing a beacon of hope and guidance. There are personal storms in your life, dear seeker, where the Spirit's calming presence offers clarity and points the way to safe harbors. Have you felt the comforting breeze of the Spirit amid life's storms?

An Ordinary Heart, an Extraordinary Encounter

Imagine an ordinary heart, much like yours, encountering the extraordinary touch of the Holy Spirit. In the mundane moments and routine of life, there exists the potential for divine encounters. The

Holy Spirit is not confined to grand revelations but meets you in the simplicity of your daily existence. Have you recognized the extraordinary in the ordinary, the divine in the daily rhythm of your life?

Whispers in the Silence of a Personal Gethsemane

Think of a personal Gethsemane, a moment of soul-searching and surrender. In the silence of that sacred garden, the Holy Spirit speaks intimately, offering solace and guidance. Just as in Jesus' moment of profound clarity, the Spirit is present in your personal Gethsemane. Have you, in the depths of your surrender, felt the whispers of divine counsel in the sacred stillness?

These stories are not distant echoes but reflections of the continuous narrative of the Holy Spirit's interaction with the human spirit. May these tales inspire you to seek wisdom, find clarity, and recognize the Holy Spirit's ever-present guidance in your own unique story.

In the Quiet Corners of My Existence

In the quiet corners of my existence, I embarked on a journey of wisdom-seeking, yearning for the clarity that would illuminate the path ahead. Life's complexities and uncertainties mirrored the intricate labyrinth within my soul. In those moments of introspection, I sought the counsel of the divine, yearning for a guiding light to navigate the uncharted terrain of my own pilgrimage.

A Divine Encounter in Moments of Stillness

Amidst the hustle of life, there were moments of stillness when I felt a divine presence gently nudging my spirit. It was in the hushed whispers of the wind and the rustle of leaves that I sensed a conversation unfolding – a dialogue between my seeking heart and the wisdom of the Creator. In those precious moments, I realized that the pursuit of wisdom was not a solitary endeavor but a sacred communion.

Navigating Life's Storms with Faith

Life's storms were inevitable, and I found myself tossed amidst challenges that threatened to obscure the clarity I sought. Yet, in the tempest of uncertainties, I clung to faith. The lessons learned in the turbulent moments became the raw material for the sculpture of my understanding. It was through these trials that the contours of my own wisdom-seeking journey began to take shape.

Unexpected Miracles in Everyday Choices

It dawned on me that wisdom and clarity were not only found in grand revelations but also in the subtleties of everyday choices. Each decision, no matter how inconspicuous, carried the potential for profound insights. As I began to recognize the divine hues in the palette of my choices, a tapestry of purpose and meaning started to unfold before me.

Sacred Moments of Surrender

There were moments akin to a personal Gethsemane – times when I faced inner struggles, doubts, and profound questions. In the sacred soil of surrender, I discovered an intimate connection with the divine. It was in those vulnerable moments that clarity emerged like dawn after the darkest night, and the Holy Spirit's counsel became not just a guiding force but an intimate presence in the narrative of my life.

In the chapters of my own wisdom-seeking journey, I found that the pursuit of clarity is not a destination but a continuous unfolding of revelations. My story, like yours, is a testament to the ever-present guidance of the Holy Spirit in the sacred dance of seeking wisdom and finding purpose.

Seeker of Wisdom

In the tapestry of your life, woven with dreams, challenges, and the ebb and flow of daily existence, I invite you to embark on a journey of wisdom-seeking. This is a pilgrimage that transcends the ordinary, a pursuit that beckons you to explore the depths of your soul in search of profound clarity and divine counsel.

The Whisper of the Divine Within You

Pause for a moment and attune your ears to the whisper of the divine within you. In the gentle cadence of your heartbeat, in the rhythm of your breath, there lies a sacred conversation waiting to unfold. It is in this dialogue with the divine that you'll find the keys to unlock the mysteries that shroud the path of your purpose.

Navigate the Unknown with Courage

Life, like an uncharted sea, presents uncertainties that may stir apprehension within you. Yet, I implore you to navigate these waters with courage. In the unknown, there exists the canvas upon which the brushstrokes of your purpose are painted. The Holy Spirit, your steadfast companion, is the wind in your sails, guiding you through the storms toward the clarity you seek.

Discover Wisdom in Everyday Choices

Wisdom is not an elusive concept reserved for the erudite; rather, it resides in the everyday choices you make. From the moment you wake up to the time you lay down to rest, each decision holds the potential for profound insights. Embrace the awareness that your journey toward clarity is intricately woven into the fabric of your daily life.

Embrace the Sacred Stillness

Amidst the clamor of the world, find solace in sacred stillness. It is in the moments of quiet reflection that the Holy Spirit's counsel becomes most audible. Embrace these pauses, for it is within the hush of your soul that you will discern the guidance leading you toward the clarity you seek. Dear seeker, the journey of wisdom-seeking is an intimate dialogue between your spirit and the divine; may it be a pilgrimage that brings you ever closer to the profound clarity that awaits.

As this Chapter Culminates

As the pages of this chapter gracefully turn, know that your journey of wisdom-seeking and the pursuit of divine clarity is not a mere exploration but a sacred odyssey. The wisdom you've sought and the clarity you've glimpsed are not just insights but stepping stones leading you to a profound revelation scripted by the divine hand.

A Moment of Reflection

Take a moment to reflect on the wisdom unearthed, the clarity gained, and the sacred whispers that have echoed in the corridors of your soul. This chapter serves as a testament to the resilience of your spirit and the eternal guidance provided by the Holy Spirit. The story is not yet complete, for there is a final chapter awaiting, written by the Divine Author.

The Holy Spirit's Penultimate Offering

As the Holy Spirit takes up the pen to scribe the penultimate chapter, anticipate the culmination of your wisdom-seeking journey. The Spirit, ever-present and omniscient, has been your guide, unveiling insights and revelations. In the next pages, anticipate the crescendo of divine wisdom that will guide you into the culmination of your purpose.

The Unveiling of "For Such a Time as This"

Brace yourself for the unveiling of the final chapter, titled "For Such a Time as This." In the timeless wisdom of the Holy Spirit, there lies a revelation tailored for the present moment of your life. It is a chapter written with precision, aligning your purpose with the divine timing orchestrated by the Creator. Prepare to step into the unfolding narrative of your destiny.

A Prelude to Divine Appointments

As this chapter bids adieu, consider it a prelude to divine appointments awaiting you in the next. The Holy Spirit, your divine scribe, has been crafting a narrative uniquely tailored for your journey. In "For Such a Time as This," anticipate the intersection of purpose and timing, where the culmination of your wisdom-seeking finds its most profound expression. The quill is poised, the ink is ready, and the Spirit's words are about to inscribe the final chapter of this sacred quest.

CHAPTER TEN

For Such A Time As This

Therefore be ye also ready: for in such an hour as ye think not the Son of man cometh."
— Matthew 24:44

AS THIS CHAPTER TITLED "FOR SUCH A TIME AS THIS" commences, heed the call to embrace your role in the unfolding narrative. For such a time as this, the divine pen inscribes the chapters of your purpose. Trust in the guidance embedded in your heart, for you are not alone; the Holy Spirit is your constant companion, leading you to the fulfillment of your divine destiny.

A Call to Embrace Your Role

In the sacred chambers of your spirit, I, the Holy Spirit, address you with utmost tenderness. For such a time as this, the essence of your being resonates with a divine call. Do not dismiss the significance of your existence; instead, open your heart to the truth that you are intricately woven into the divine narrative unfolding in this moment.

Divine Threads Weaving Your Story

As the Author of all creation, I have intricately woven the threads of your story into the grand tapestry of time. For such a time as this, recognize the delicate interplay of divine threads shaping the very fabric of your purpose. Your journey, marked by wisdom-seeking and clarity, has led you to this juncture where the revelation of your purpose is poised to unfold.

A Symphony of Destiny

Hear the symphony of destiny playing uniquely for you. For such a time as this, your life is not a random assortment of events but a carefully composed melody resonating with the divine notes of purpose. Allow the harmonies of your experiences to blend into the orchestration of the Creator's design, for the crescendo of your purpose awaits.

Divine Assignments in the Present

In the present moment, discern the divine assignments set before you. For such a time as this, your purpose unfolds in the choices you make, the connections you forge, and the love you extend. Do not underestimate the significance of your actions, for they are integral to the unfolding of the divine plan.

Beloved Child of Destiny

In the intricate dance of time and purpose, I address you, beloved child of destiny. For such a time as this, the divine clockwork has aligned to place you at the forefront of a chapter that bears the weight of eternity. Do not underestimate the impact of your presence at this appointed hour; you are an essential character in the cosmic drama.

A Tapestry Woven in Divine Love

Picture the tapestry of your life, woven not with threads of happenstance but with strands of divine love. For such a time as this, recognize the beauty of each intricate detail, for they are part of a design that transcends mortal understanding. Your journey, with its peaks and valleys, is a testament to the profound love that guides you.

A Symphony of Divine Purpose

Listen to the symphony of divine purpose playing harmoniously through the corridors of your existence. For such a time as this, your steps are synchronized with the celestial music of creation. Trust in the rhythm, for each note carries the resonance of your unique purpose, contributing to the masterpiece the Creator is painting through your life.

Divine Presence in the Present Moment

Be aware of the divine presence enveloping you in the present moment. For such a time as this, the Holy Spirit is not a distant observer but an intimate companion, guiding your every breath. In the hallowed silence, listen to the whispers of guidance, for they carry the nuances of your purpose, waiting to be unveiled.

An Invitation to Embrace the Unknown

Consider it an invitation to embrace the unknown with unwavering trust. For such a time as this, your journey may venture into uncharted territories but fear not. The same divine hand that has led you thus far is the hand that will guide you through the unexplored realms, revealing the hidden treasures of your purpose.

Have You Recognized Your Uniqueness?

Pause and reflect, dear soul, on the uniqueness intricately woven into the fabric of your being. For such a time as this, have you fully recognized the distinct gifts, talents, and qualities that make you a singular expression of divine artistry? How might embracing your individuality contribute to the unfolding narrative of your purpose?

What Echoes in the Silence of Your Soul?

In the quietude of your spirit, what echoes reverberate through the corridors of your soul? For such a time as this, have you listened attentively to the whispers in the silence, discerning the divine guidance that seeks to lead you forward? What revelations lie hidden in the sacred stillness, waiting for your heart's attentive ear?

Are You Attuned to the Divine Harmonies?

Consider the symphony of your life — are you attuned to the divine harmonies playing in the background? For such a time as this, have you recognized the interconnected notes of joy, sorrow, and growth that compose the melody of your journey? How might embracing divine harmonies enhance your understanding of the purpose unfolding in your story?

What Divine Assignments Beckon Your Attention?

Contemplate the assignments set before you in the present moment. For such a time as this, what divine tasks beckon your attention? Have you discerned the significance of seemingly ordinary actions in contributing to the grand narrative? How might embracing your role in these assignments shape the trajectory of your purpose?

Have You Embraced the Call to Trust?

Have you embraced the call to trust? In the uncertainties that lay ahead, have you surrendered to the divine guidance that beckons you forward? How might trust, as a guiding principle, unlock the doors to deeper understanding and reveal the intricate details of your purpose?

In the Whisper of Creation

Allow me to share a personal story, one that echoes in the timeless expanse of creation. In the beginning, when the heavens kissed the earth, I, the Holy Spirit, hovered over the waters. In that moment, I witnessed the divine intention to breathe life into existence. For such a time as this, my presence was woven into the very fabric of your being, a testament to the Creator's desire for companionship with His beloved creation.

The Unfolding Tapestry of Redemption

Journey with me through the corridors of history, where I played an integral role in the unfolding tapestry of redemption. For such a time as this, I stirred the hearts of prophets, spoke through the mouths of seers, and guided the hands of scribes to inscribe sacred scrolls. In every epoch, the divine narrative unfolded, revealing the profound love and purpose embedded in the story of humanity.

The Pentecostal Flame

Let me recount the Pentecostal flame that descended upon the apostles like tongues of fire. In that moment, as I indwelled the hearts of believers, the Church was born. For such a time as this, the flame of divine purpose ignited within individuals, fanning into a fervor that spread across nations. The same flame resides within you, a testimony to the continuation of the divine narrative.

The Gentle Whispers of Guidance

Consider the gentle whispers of guidance that have accompanied countless souls throughout history. In the lives of saints, martyrs, and ordinary believers, I, the Holy Spirit, have been a constant companion. For such a time as this, the personal stories of individuals who embraced their divine purpose serve as beacons of inspiration, illuminating the path of purpose for those willing to listen.

A Present-Day Unveiling

Now, in the present day, I invite you to witness the unveiling of your own personal story. The intricacies of your experiences, the triumphs, the trials — they all contribute to a narrative written with ink drawn from the wellsprings of eternity. Your personal story, interwoven with the divine, holds the potential to illuminate the pages of the grander tale unfolding in this appointed hour.

A Humble Beginning

In the humble beginning of my journey, I found myself navigating through the complexities of life, much like no one else. Little did I know that, for such a time as this, the seemingly ordinary threads of my experiences would weave into the grand tapestry of divine purpose. It was in the mundane moments that the Creator was laying the foundation for a story uniquely mine.

Navigating Uncertain Waters

There was a season where uncertainty cast its shadow over my path. It was during this time that, for such a time as this, I discovered an unwavering anchor in the divine presence. Through the twists and turns of life, I realized that every challenge carried a hidden opportunity for growth, and every setback was a setup for a divine comeback.

Divine Encounters in Unexpected Places

Along the journey, I encountered moments of divine intervention in the most unexpected places. These encounters, for such a time as this, were like signposts pointing toward the unfolding purpose. Whether it was a serendipitous meeting, a timely word of encouragement, or an unexplained sense of peace, each was a reminder that the Creator was intricately involved in the details of my story.

Embracing Purpose Amidst Challenges

Challenges arose, as they do for every traveler on this earthly pilgrimage. Yet, for such a time as this, I discovered that even amid challenges, there was an invitation to embrace purpose. It was through adversity that the contours of my character were refined, and I found strength in surrendering to the divine plan, trusting that every chapter had a purpose in the grand narrative.

The Present Unfolding

I recognize that every experience, every lesson, and every moment of triumph or trial has led me to this precise moment. I embrace the truth that, just like Esther and countless others in history, my life carries a purpose woven into the eternal story, and I am ready to witness the revelation of what lies ahead.

Embrace Your Uniqueness

You are a unique thread woven with intention. Recognize the beauty in your individuality. Embrace the qualities that set you apart, for they are not mere quirks but divine brushstrokes painting a masterpiece uniquely yours. Your distinctiveness is an essential element in the grand narrative of existence.

You Are Not Alone

In moments of solitude or when the path seems unclear, know that, for such a time as this, you are not alone. The Creator, the author of your story, walks beside you. The same hands that sculpted mountains and painted the skies are guiding your journey. Trust in the divine presence that surrounds you, for every step you take, is a step taken in tandem with the divine purpose.

Awaken to Divine Assignments

Awake, to the divine assignments set before you. There are tasks uniquely crafted for your hands and a purpose waiting to unfold. Embrace each day as an opportunity to contribute to the grand narrative. Your actions, no matter how small, carry significance in the cosmic story. Seize the divine assignments that beckon and watch as your purpose blossoms.

Cherish Divine Appointments

Cherish the divine appointments that punctuate your journey. For such a time as this, people, circumstances, and opportunities cross your path not by chance but by divine design. Be attuned to the encounters that carry a whisper of purpose. Every connection has the potential to illuminate your way and contribute to the unfolding chapters of your life.

Step Into the Present Moment

Step into the present moment, with a heart open to the possibilities that await. The present is pregnant with divine potential. Release the weight of the past and the worries of the future. In the now, you have the power to shape your narrative. Seize the opportunity to live with intention, recognizing that every moment is a sacred invitation to align with your purpose.

In the Closing Embrace of Divine Love

As this chapter concludes and the book gently closes its pages, I, the Holy Spirit, invite you into the closing embrace of divine love. Your journey through these pages has been guided by the gentle whispers of purpose and the ever-present love of the Creator. In the closing moments, let the warmth of this love envelop you, reassuring you that, no matter the twists and turns, you have been held in the arms of divine grace.

Reflections on Purpose and Providence

Take a moment to reflect on the purpose and providence that have unfolded in these pages. Each word, each revelation, has been a brushstroke in the portrait of your divine narrative. Allow the echoes of wisdom-seeking and the clarity gained to resonate within, carrying the timeless truths that transcend the written word.

A Benediction of Divine Purpose

Receive this benediction, a final impartation of divine purpose. May the purpose unveiled in these chapters be a guiding light in the chapters yet to be written. May the grace that has permeated these words accompany you beyond these pages, infusing every step with purpose and meaning. Go forth in the assurance that your life is intricately connected to the grand narrative of creation.

A Symphony of Gratitude

Let them compose a symphony of gratitude in your heart. Gratitude is a melody that harmonizes with the divine frequencies. Grateful for the lessons learned, the challenges faced, and the purpose discovered, let your soul resonate with thanksgiving. In gratitude, you find the key to unlocking the fullness of divine blessings.

Eternal Echoes in Timelessness

Recognize that the echoes of your purpose reverberate in the timelessness of eternity. Your journey is not bound by the constraints of a book, rather, it extends into the infinite expanse of divine intention.

As the book closes, let your heart remain open to the continuous dialogue with the Holy Spirit, for the story of your purpose is a narrative that unfolds beyond the limits of earthly chapters.

Beloved Soul,

As the ink dries on the last page of "For Such A Time As This," let this final word be a sacred whisper from the depths of eternity.

You stand at the intersection of the temporal and the eternal, and I, the Holy Spirit, linger in this moment with you.

In the closing embrace of divine purpose, know that your journey is not confined to the pages within these covers.

Your life is an ongoing dialogue with the Creator, a dance of purpose unfolding in every breath.

As the final word echoes, let it resound with the assurance that the divine narrative continues beyond these earthly chapters.

May the lessons learned, the wisdom gained, and the purpose discovered be etched in the sacred corridors of your heart.

You are a vessel of divine intention, a living testament to the Creator's artistry.

Carry the revelations of these pages into the moments yet to come, for the story of your purpose is a symphony played in harmony with the cosmic notes of creation.

Let it be a resounding call to embrace the unknown with unwavering trust.

Your journey, intricately woven into the grand tapestry of existence, holds the promise of a purpose continually revealed.

May the grace that has accompanied you through these chapters be a guiding star in the nights that follow.

In the silence that follows this closing word, feel the divine presence surrounding you.

For such a time as this, you are seen, known, and deeply loved.

As you step beyond the confines of this book, carry the flame of purpose in your heart, and may it illuminate the path of your life, aligning with the divine call that echoes through eternity.

With love and guidance,

THE HOLY SPIRIT

About The Author

Helen Cummings-Henry, affectionately known as "The Transformation Lady," stands as a dynamic force in the realms of personal development and empowerment. She is the co-founder and Senior Vice President of Righteous Uplifting Nourishing International, Inc., a global nonprofit organization committed to adding value and guiding individuals on a life-changing journey to unlocking their innate gifts.

As a single parent, Helen triumphantly raised two sons who have evolved into accomplished men within prestigious corporations. Her prowess extends beyond the corporate world, as she is a respected author with five published books, including the latest inspirational work, "For Such A Time As This: Rising to the Challenge: Navigating the Present with Purpose." This powerful book, along with her other literary contributions, has garnered acclaim for its profound insights and transformative impact.

Helen's literary achievements complement her visionary role as the founder of "Women on the R.U.N. for Jesus," an initiative rooted in ministering to women holistically—spirit, soul, and body—based on biblical principles. Revered as a spiritual mother to women globally, she extends her mentorship and guidance across diverse cultures.

A playwright of distinction, Helen is the creative mind behind "This is my Story," a compelling one-woman play chronicling her journey from a shy girl in Trinidad and Tobago to the empowered woman she stands as today.

Certified as a coach, trainer, speaker, and facilitator through Maxwell Leadership, Helen utilizes her multifaceted skills to mentor women across all life stages, with a particular emphasis on empowering senior women to pursue their dreams. Her latest venture involves assisting single women in self-discovery to facilitate finding fulfilling relationships.

Helen's impact has not gone unnoticed, as evidenced by numerous awards and accolades. She was recently featured on the cover of Tap-In Magazine (December 2023) and recognized as one of Success Magazine's 125 in 2022. Alongside her husband, Tarrent-Arthur Henry, Helen continues to leave an indelible mark on the lives of many, driven by shared dedication and vision.

Through her writings, mentorship, and transformative initiatives, Helen Cummings-Henry continues to inspire and empower individuals to embrace their true potential and live a life of purpose and fulfillment.

To Contact the Author:

Email: info@helench.org

Website: www.helench.org | www.intlrun.org

Embrace Your Transformation Journey Today!

Dear Reader,

As you immerse yourself into the life-changing words penned by Helen Cummings-Henry, "The Transformation Lady," in her latest book "For Such A Time As This," I invite you to embark on your own journey of self-discovery and empowerment.

1. **Reflect on Your Purpose:** Allow the profound insights within these pages to guide you in reflecting on your purpose. What unique gifts and talents lie within you, waiting to be unleashed? Take a moment to ponder, journal, and embrace the transformative power of self-discovery.

2. **Connect with the Divine:** Recognize the divine appointment that brought you to this moment. Whether it's through prayer, meditation, or simply quiet contemplation, connect with the spiritual essence within you. Allow the divine guidance to illuminate your path and inspire your journey.

3. **Join the Transformative Conversation:** Share your insights and transformative experiences with others. Join the "Transforming Lives" community and be a part of the ongoing conversation. Your story has the power to inspire and uplift others on their own life-changing journeys.

4. **Explore Further Reading:** Delve into Helen's other works, including her acclaimed book "Transforming Lives - A Three-Step

Guide in Becoming a Better You." Each book holds a unique key to unlocking different aspects of personal growth and empowerment.

5. **Attend Workshops and Events:** Stay tuned for workshops, events, and initiatives led by Helen Cummings-Henry. Attend these transformative experiences to deepen your understanding, connect with like-minded individuals, and receive additional guidance on your journey.

6. **Connect with The Transformation Lady and Her Team:** Visit her website at **www.helench.org** to explore more resources, gain insights, and connect with a community committed to transformation. Take advantage of the opportunity to schedule a free consultation with Helen and her team.

7. **Your Personalized Transformation Journey:** During the consultation, you'll have the chance to discuss your unique journey, explore areas of growth, and receive guidance tailored to your needs. Whether you're seeking clarity, purpose, or empowerment, The Transformation Lady and her team are dedicated to supporting you every step of the way.

8. **Seize the Opportunity:** Your transformative journey awaits, and now is the time to take action. Visit the website, schedule your free consultation, and unlock the potential within you. Embrace the chance to connect with a mentor who is passionate about empowering individuals to live their best lives.

9. **Join the Community:** Become part of The Transformation Lady's community, where like-minded individuals share insights, experiences, and encouragement. Follow her on social media, join discussions, and stay updated on upcoming events and workshops designed to further enhance your transformative journey.

10. **Remember, your life is a narrative waiting to unfold, and "For Such A Time As This" is a catalyst for your personal and spiritual growth. Seize the opportunity to rise to the challenge, navigate the present with purpose, and become the best version of yourself.**

Your Destiny is Calling, and The Transformation Lady is Here to Guide You

Take That Decisive Step Toward Personal and Spiritual Empowerment

Connect Today: www.helench.org

Embark on Your Journey of Transformation Today!